89383

D1308301

DISCOVERING CAREERS FOR YOUR FUTURE

math

SECOND EDITION

Ferguson
An imprint of Infobase Publishing

Discovering Careers for Your Future: Math, Second Edition

Copyright © 2008 by Infobase Publishing

Ferguson
An imprint of Infobase Publishing
132 West 31st Street
New York NY 10001

Library of Congress Cataloging-in-Publication Data

Discovering careers for your future. Math. — 2nd ed.
   p. cm.
   Includes bibliographical references and index.
   ISBN-13: 978-0-8160-7278-1 (hardcover : alk. paper)
   ISBN-10: 0-8160-7278-7 (hardcover : alk. paper)
Vocational guidance—Juvenile literature. I. J.G. Ferguson Publishing Company.
   QA10.5.D57 2008
   510.23—dc22

                    2007040865

Ferguson books are available at special discounts when purchased in bulk quantities for businesses, associations, institutions, or sales promotions. Please call our Special Sales Department in New York at (212) 967-8800 or (800) 322-8755.

You can find Ferguson on the World Wide Web at http://www.fergpubco.com.

Text design by Mary Susan Ryan-Flynn
Cover design by Jooyoung An

Printed in the United States of America

EB MSRF 10 9 8 7 6 5 4 3 2 1

This book is printed on acid-free paper.

Contents

Introduction

You may not have decided yet what you want to be in the future. And you do not have to decide right away. You do know that right now you are interested in mathematics. Do any of the statements below describe you? If so, you may want to begin thinking about what a career in math might mean for you.

___Math is my favorite subject in school.

___I like to work on math problems.

___I like number games.

___I like strategy games, such as chess.

___I like computers.

___I keep careful track of my money.

___I am curious about how things work.

___I am good at observing details.

___I like to solve problems.

___I like science.

___I like to take things apart and see if I can put them back together.

___I like to invent things.

Discovering Careers for Your Future: Math is a book about careers in math, from actuaries to math teachers. Math is important in dozens of careers in government, science, business, and industry. Computers, banking and finance, and engineering are all based on mathematics.

This book describes many possibilities for future careers that math. Read through it and see how different math careers are connected. For example, if you are interested in money and banking, you will want to read the chapters on accountants, actuaries, bank services workers, bookkeepers, and financial planners. If you are interested in computers, you will want to read the chapters on computer systems analysts, software designers, and software engineers. If you are interested in applying your interest in math to careers in engineering and the construction industry, you will want to check out the chapters on engineering technicians, engineers, and surveyors. Or perhaps you are interested in space careers, so you will want to check out the articles on astronomers and physicists. Go ahead and explore!

What Do Math Specialists Do?

The first section of each chapter begins with a heading such as "What Demographers Do" or "What Statisticians Do." It tells what it's like to work at a particular job. It describes typical responsibilities and assignments. You will find out about working conditions. Do people in a particular field work in offices or laboratories? Do they use computers? What other tools and equipment do they use? This section answers all these questions.

How Do I Become a Math Specialist?

The section called "Education and Training" tells you what schooling you need for employment in each job—a high school diploma, training at a junior college, a college degree, or more. It also talks about on-the-job training that you could expect to receive after you're hired and whether or not you must complete an apprenticeship program.

How Much Do Math Specialists Earn?

The "Earnings" section gives the average salary figures for the job described in the chapter. These figures provide you with a general idea of how much money people with this job can make. Keep in mind that many people really earn more or less than the amounts given here because actual salaries depend on many factors, such as the size of the company, the location of the company, and the amount of education, training, and experience you have. Generally, but not always, bigger companies located in major cities pay more than smaller ones in smaller cities and towns, and people with more education, training, and experience earn more. Also remember that these figures are current averages. They will probably be different by the time you are ready to enter the workforce.

What Will the Future Be Like for Math Specialists?

The Outlook section discusses the employment outlook for the career: Whether the total number of people employed in this career will increase or decrease in the coming years and whether jobs in this field will be easy or hard to find. These predictions are based on economic conditions, the size and makeup of the population, foreign competition, and new technology. Terms such as "faster than the average," "about as fast as the average," and "more slowly than the average" are used by the U.S. Department of Labor, a government agency that collects data about the world of work, to describe job growth.

Keep in mind that these predictions are general statements. No one knows for sure what the future will be like. Also remember that the employment outlook is a general statement about an industry and does not necessarily apply to everyone. A determined and talented person may be able to find a job in an industry or career with the worst kind of outlook. And a person without ambition and the proper training will find it difficult to find a job in even a booming industry or career field.

Where Can I Find More Information?

Each chapter includes a sidebar called "For More Info." It lists organizations that you can contact to find out more about the field and careers in the field. You will find names, addresses, phone numbers, e-mail addresses, and Web sites of math-oriented associations and organizations.

Extras

Every chapter has a few extras. There are photos that show math workers in action. There are sidebars and notes on ways to explore the field, lists of recommended personal and professional qualities, fun facts, profiles of people in the field, and lists of Web sites and books that might be helpful. At the end of the book you will find three additional sections: Glossary, Browse and Learn More, and Index. The Glossary gives brief definitions of words that relate to education, career training, or employment that may be unfamiliar to you. The Browse and Learn More section lists general math books and Web sites to explore. The Index includes all the job titles mentioned in the book.

It's not too soon to think about your future. We hope you discover several possible career choices. Happy hunting!

Accountants

What Accountants Do

Accountants are numbers people. They are in charge of all of the financial records of an individual, business, or other organization. For example, accountants hired by a company add and subtract how much the company makes and spends over a given period of a time, such as a month. They calculate how much money is spent on operating costs. Examples of operating costs are bills for electricity, rent, and the use and repair of office equipment, such as computers. Accountants also measure a company's revenue, which is how much money comes in through the sales of products or services.

An accountant for a bakery, for example, would assess how much was spent to pay the workers, how much was spent to operate the bakery ovens, and how much was spent to buy the ingredients to make the bread and other products. These costs are called debits and are subtracted from the company's bank account. Then the accountant would calculate the money coming in from the sales of bread, cookies, cakes, and other goods the bakery sells. After the books are closed for each accounting period (such as a month), the accountant prepares reports that will indicate whether or not a profit was made for that time period. These reports are then presented to the president or owner of the company so he or she can make

Accounting Glossary

If you are confused about the meaning of accounting terms such as *business valuation*, *disclosure*, and *issue papers*, the American Institute of Certified Public Accountants has a useful glossary of terms at its Web site, http://www.aicpa.org/download/mediacenter/AICPA_Glossary.pdf. It details more than 230 accounting terms, federal laws, and government entities.

EXPLORING

○ Learn more about this career by checking out books at your local library and exploring accounting association Web sites.

○ Keeping the financial records of a school club is an excellent way to explore the work of accountants.

○ Get a job in a retail business, either part-time or during the summer. Working at the cash register or even pricing products as a stockperson is good introductory experience.

decisions about how to operate the business during the immediate and long-term future.

Accountants not only review financial records, they also set up systems to keep track of the way money is handled. For example, if a company does not have an employee who records expenses and income on a daily basis, an accountant might create such a bookkeeping system. Accountants often use computers to help keep track of financial records and solve mathematical problems.

Education And Training

If you are considering a career as an accountant, you should be good at mathematics and enjoy working with numbers. In high school, take classes in mathematics and English, as well as bookkeeping and other business courses.

To Be a Successful Accountant, You Should . . .

○ love mathematics and working with numbers

○ have strong mathematical, analytical, and problem-solving skills

○ be able to think logically and to interpret facts and figures accurately

○ have excellent oral and written communication skills

Mean Annual Earnings for Accountants by Industry, 2006

Federal Executive Branch	$79,340
Accounting, Tax Preparation, Bookkeeping, and Payroll Services	$66,990
Management of Companies and Enterprises	$59,920
Depository Credit Intermediation	$54,690
Local Government	$52,420
State Government	$49,100

Source: U.S. Department of Labor

A college education with a major in accounting is the best way to prepare to be an accountant. Private business schools, junior colleges, and some technical schools also offer training programs. In these programs, students take courses in mathematics, accounting methods, and computers. Although any type of training in accounting is valuable, people with a college degree will usually find higher-paying jobs. Many accountants also pass a state examination and obtain a license to practice as certified public accountants.

Earnings

Accountants earned average salaries of $54,630 in 2006, according to the U.S. Department of Labor. Some accountants made as little as $34,070, while others earned more than $94,050.

Outlook

The job outlook for skilled accountants through the next decade is bright. More and more professionals will be needed to check the financial records of businesses and other organizations. Some accountants will work for banks and large companies, and others will work on their own. Many accountants, especially certified public accountants, will help people with their tax returns.

FOR MORE INFO

For industry information, contact
**American Institute of
Certified Public
Accountants**
1211 Avenue of the Americas
New York, NY 10036-8775
Tel: 212-596-6200
http://www.aicpa.org

*For information on accredited programs
in accounting, contact*
**The Association to Advance
Collegiate Schools of
Business**
777 South Harbour Island Boulevard
Suite 750
Tampa, FL 33602-5730
Tel: 813-769-6500
http://www.aacsb.edu

*For information on women in accounting,
contact*
**The Educational Foundation for
Women in Accounting**
PO Box 1925
Southeastern, PA 19399-1925
Tel: 610-407-9229
E-mail: info@efwa.org
http://www.efwa.org

*For information about management
accounting and certification, contact*
**Institute of Management
Accountants**
10 Paragon Drive
Montvale, NJ 07645-1718
Tel: 800-638-4427
E-mail: ima@imanet.org
http://www.imanet.org

Actuaries

What Actuaries Do

Actuaries are mathematicians who design and plan insurance and pension programs for businesses. They make mathematical calculations to help insurance companies figure out how much money they may have to pay to the businesses and workers they insure. They also figure out how much the policies should cost.

Insurance policies are formal agreements between insurance companies and policyholders. The policyholder pays a certain amount of money for the policy. This is usually a monthly fee called a premium. In return, the insurance company agrees to pay money to policyholders if they later suffer certain financial losses, such as those caused by accidents, illness, unemployment, or death. For example, if an insurance policyholder has a car accident, he or she files a claim with the insurance company. The claim shows the cost of the accident, including the cost to repair damage to the car or the amount of doctor bills to treat injuries. Insurance companies have created many different kinds of insurance, including life, medical, automobile, fire, and unemployment insurance. Many insurance companies may also handle pension programs. Pension is money paid to a worker after retirement.

Where Do Actuaries Work?

These are the most common places where actuaries work:

○ insurance industry—property (home) and casualty (car)
○ life and annuities
○ employee benefits
○ pensions
○ health
○ Social Security
○ financial industry
○ banks, investing, risk management

Source: Casualty Actuarial Society

EXPLORING

○ If you think you are interested in becoming an actuary, try activities that allow you to develop strategies and to practice problem-solving skills. For example, you might join the school chess club, math club, or investment club.

○ Participate in activities that teach you leadership and management, such as student council.

○ Visit the Web sites of colleges and universities that offer actuarial science programs to learn more about educational requirements.

Actuaries try to predict the number of policyholders who will have losses and how much money the insurance company will have to pay in claims. They then help the insurance company set prices for policies so that it will always have enough money to pay all the claims.

Actuaries use their knowledge of mathematics, probability, statistics, and principles of finance and business. Usually they begin by collecting and studying facts on events such as births, deaths, marriage, and employment. They then make tables to show the rates at which deaths, accidents, sickness, disability, or retirement occur. For example, when they set the cost for earthquake insurance, actuaries look at how often earthquakes happen in the homeowner's area. If the owner lives in California, the insurance is going to cost more than for someone who lives in Kansas, because California has so many more earthquakes than Kansas. But the tornado insurance for a Kansas home will cost more than for a home in

The Benefits of Becoming an Actuary

○ good pay and benefits

○ excellent job security

○ gaining skills you can use in other careers

○ working in an exciting and dynamic career field

Source: BeAnActuary.org

It's a Fact

The term *actuary* was used for the first time in 1762 in the charter for the Equitable Society of London, the first life insurance company to use scientific data in figuring premiums. The basis of actuarial work started when French mathematicians Blaise Pascal (1623–1662) and Pierre de Fermat (1601–1665) figured out a way to calculate actuarial probabilities. Their work resulted in what is now called the science of probability.

The first mortality table was produced when Edmund Halley (1656–1742) noticed that there were more male births than female births. Halley is known as the father of life insurance and he is also the English astronomer for whom Halley's Comet is named.

In 1889, a small group of actuaries formed the Actuarial Society of America. Two classes of members—fellows and associates—were created seven years later, and special examinations were developed to determine membership eligibility. By 1909, the American Institute of Actuaries was created, and in 1949 these two groups joined into the present Society of Actuaries.

California, because Kansas has a lot of tornadoes and California does not.

Education and Training

To be an actuary, you must like math and be able to do careful, detailed work. In high school you should take as much mathematics (especially calculus) as possible. Computer science training is also important. After high school, you will have to go to college to earn a bachelor's degree in mathematics or statistics.

Employers prefer to hire actuaries who have successfully passed a series of special examinations. The first two of these examinations should be taken while still in college. Actuaries

FOR MORE INFO

For general information about actuary careers, contact
American Academy of Actuaries
1100 17th Street NW, Seventh Floor
Washington, DC 20036-4601
Tel: 202-223-8196
http://www.actuary.org

The "Be An Actuary" section of the CAS's Web site offers comprehensive information on actuary careers.
Casualty Actuarial Society (CAS)
4350 North Fairfax Drive, Suite 250
Arlington, VA 22203-1695
Tel: 703-276-3100
E-mail: office@casact.org
http://www.beanactuary.org

For industry information, contact
Society of Actuaries
475 North Martingale Road, Suite 600
Schaumburg, IL 60173
Tel: 847-706-3500
http://www.soa.org

usually take the other exams after they start working.

Earnings

Starting salaries for actuaries with bachelor's degrees in actuarial science averaged $52,741 in 2005, according to the National Association of Colleges and Employers. New college graduates who have not passed any actuarial examinations earn slightly less. Insurance companies and consulting firms offer merit increases or bonuses to those who pass examinations.

The U.S. Department of Labor reports that actuaries earned a median annual salary of $82,800 in 2006. Salaries ranged from less than $46,470 to more than $114,570.

Outlook

Employment for actuaries is expected to grow about as fast as the average. The field's demanding entrance requirements and competition for entry-level jobs will also continue to limit the number of candidates for jobs.

Astronomers

What Astronomers Do

Astronomers study the universe and all the celestial, or cosmic, bodies in space. They use telescopes, computers, and complex measuring tools to find the positions of stars and planets. They calculate the orbits of comets, asteroids, and artificial satellites. They study how celestial objects form and deteriorate, and they try to figure out how the universe started.

With special equipment, astronomers collect and analyze information about planets and stars, such as temperature, shape, size, brightness, and motion. They use this knowledge to help scientists know when to launch a space vehicle or a satellite. The astronomer's work also helps other scientists to better understand space, the origins of the Earth and the universe, and the atmosphere surrounding the Earth.

Astronomers usually specialize in one area of study. For example, *stellar astronomers* study the stars. *Solar astronomers* study the Sun. *Planetary astronomers* study conditions on the planets. *Cosmologists* study the origin and the structure of the universe and *astrophysicists* study the physical and chemical changes that occur in the universe. *Celestial mechanics specialists* study the motion and position of planets and other objects in the solar system. *Radio astronomers* study the source

Did You Know?

○ The Earth is about 93 million miles away from the Sun.

○ The Sun is so large that you could fit one million Earths inside.

○ The Moon is one-quarter Earth's size.

○ In the daytime, the Moon's mean temperature is 225°F. At night, its mean temperature is −243°F.

○ Asteroids can be as tiny as a pebble. The largest known asteroid is Ceres. It is about 597 miles in diameter.

Source: Astronomy.com

13

EXPLORING

○ Join an amateur astronomy club. There are many such clubs all over the country. These clubs usually have telescopes and will let members view the night skies.

○ Visit a nearby planetarium and ask astronomers who work there about their jobs. Planetariums also help you learn more about the universe and see if this is a career you would like.

○ There are many astronomy sites on the Internet. Visit the National Aeronautics and Space Administration's Web site at http://www.nasa.gov. *Astronomy* magazine (http://www.astronomy.com/asy/default.aspx) also has a great site that will help you learn more about our solar system.

and nature of celestial radio waves using sensitive radio telescopes.

Most astronomers teach at universities or colleges. A few lecture at planetariums. Some work at research institutions or at observatories. Those who work at observatories spend a few nights each a month observing the sky through a telescope. They spend the rest of their time in offices or laboratories where they study, analyze their data, and write reports.

Education and Training

Training to become an astronomer can begin in high school. You should plan to take classes in mathematics, chemistry, physics, geography, and foreign languages (especially French, German, and Russian). Because astronomy is a high-technology field, you should try to learn as much as you can about computers.

Will Asteroids Strike Earth?

How likely is an asteroid to crash into Earth? Astronomers and other scientists say such an event is not very likely. The most dangerous asteroids, those capable of causing major disasters, are extremely rare, according to NASA. These objects hit Earth once every 100,000 years on average.

NASA KIDS' CLUB

The National Aeronautics and Space Administration (NASA) has a Web site especially for kids. You can learn about Earth and the other planets, space travel, the stars and galaxies, and NASA. Here's the address: http://www.nasa.gov/audience/forkids/home.

After high school, you will have to earn a bachelor's degree in physics, mathematics, or astronomy. Once you receive your bachelor's degree, you may find work as an assistant or researcher. Most astronomers go on to earn both a master's degree and a doctorate.

Earnings

Astronomers had average earnings of $95,740 in 2006, according to the U.S. Department of Labor. Salaries ranged from less than $44,590 to $125,420 or more annually. The average for astronomers employed by the federal government in 2006 was $117,350.

Outlook

Astronomy is one of the smallest science fields, so this field is very competitive. The U.S. Department of Labor says there will be fewer new jobs for astronomers in the government—except for those who are employed by defense-related agencies. The greatest growth in the field of astronomy will be in jobs in business and industry.

FOR MORE INFO

Visit the FAQ section at the following Web site to read the online article, "Career Profile: Astronomy."
American Association of Amateur Astronomers
PO Box 7981
Dallas, TX 75209-0981
http://www.astromax.com

To read "A New Universe to Discover: A Guide to Careers in Astronomy," visit the AAS's Web site.
American Astronomical Society (AAS)
2000 Florida Avenue NW, Suite 400
Washington, DC 20009-1231
Tel: 202-328-2010
E-mail: aas@aas.org
http://www.aas.org

Auditors

What Auditors Do

Auditors study the business and financial records of a company to make sure that they are correct and complete. They help the company prevent mistakes and follow the laws for company record keeping. After they examine the records, auditors give reports to the company managers and suggest ways to improve their record-keeping practices.

There are several kinds of auditors. *Internal auditors* are employees of a company. They help the company's accountants keep accurate records. They may also examine records to make sure employees are not using the company's money and property improperly. *Independent auditors* work for a separate auditing company. Businesses hire them on a temporary basis to check their records and to make sure their own auditors and accountants are accurate. Independent auditors sometimes must travel to companies in other cities. *Tax auditors* examine taxpayers' records to figure the correct amount of taxes they owe. Most tax auditors work for the state or federal government.

Education and Training

If you want to become an auditor, you must do well in math classes, even in grade school. In high school, you should continue your math studies and also take classes in business, such as

Bean Counters No More

Accountants and auditors have long been called "bean counters." Their work has been considered boring and tedious. People used to associate them with death, taxes, and bad news. But that has changed. Accountants and auditors do much more than record financial information. Computers now count the "beans" while accountants and auditors analyze the results.

bookkeeping, and computer courses. Classes in English, speech, and writing also are helpful.

To be an auditor, you must first study to become an accountant. You can find accountant training at business schools, junior colleges, colleges, and universities. You will need to earn a bachelor's degree with a major in accounting. College graduates with two years of experience in internal auditing can take an exam offered by the Institute of Internal Auditors. By passing this exam you become a certified internal auditor. After college, you will have to take more classes and pass an examination to become a certified public accountant (CPA). In most states, large public accounting firms hire only CPAs.

EXPLORING

○ Ask your parents to show you how to balance a checkbook.

○ Keep a spending diary. Write down what you buy each day and how much it costs. How much have you spent? Saved?

○ You can get accounting experience and auditing skills by volunteering to be treasurer for school clubs or organizations.

○ If your school has a fund-raising event, you could offer to keep track of the financial records.

It's a Fact

○ Accounting records and bookkeeping methods have been used since ancient times. Records discovered in Babylonia (modern-day Iraq) date back to 3600 B.C. Accounts were kept by the ancient Greeks and the Romans.

○ Modern accounting began with double-entry bookkeeping, which was developed by Luca Pacioli (c. 1450–c.1520), an Italian mathematician.

○ The accounting profession in the United States dates back only to 1880, when English and Scottish investors began to buy stock in American companies. To keep an eye on their investments, they sent over accountants. When the accountants saw the great opportunities in the accounting field, they stayed in America to establish their own businesses.

○ The U.S. government started to collect income tax in 1913.

Earnings

Auditors earn average salaries of about $54,000 a year. They start at about $34,000. Auditors' salaries vary according to their experience, the type of business that employs them, and the difficulty of the accounting systems they are auditing. More experienced auditors may earn $94,000 or more a year. Auditors who work for the federal government earn less than those in private industry.

Outlook

The need for auditors is expected to grow because businesses' accounting needs are continuing to expand. Managers rely heavily on accounting information to make business decisions.

FOR MORE INFO

For information on certification, contact
American Institute of Certified Public Accountants
1211 Avenue of the Americas
New York, NY 10036-8775
Tel: 212-596-6200
http://www.aicpa.org

Information Systems Audit and Control Association
3701 Algonquin Road, Suite 1010
Rolling Meadows, IL 60008-3124
Tel: 847-253-1545
E-mail: certification@isaca.org
http://www.isaca.org

For information on internal auditing and certification, contact
The Institute of Internal Auditors
247 Maitland Avenue
Altamonte Springs, FL 32701-4201
Tel: 407-937-1100
E-mail: iia@theiia.org
http://www.theiia.org

Bank Services Workers

What Bank Services Workers Do

A bank receives, exchanges, lends, and safeguards money. Changes in the economy and the increasing use of computers and automatic teller machines affect the banking industry and the people who work there. There are many types of workers employed in the banking industry.

Bank tellers handle certain types of customer account transactions. These employees serve the public directly. They accept customers' deposits and give them receipts. They also pay out withdrawals, record transactions, and cash checks. In addition, they make sure that there is enough money in the account to cover the check.

Bank officers and *managers* supervise workers and handle loans and other financial matters at a bank. They are responsible for directing employees, making assignments, and overseeing day-to-day operations. Bank officers might also work in accounting, public relations, advertising, or other areas of a bank. Officers review budgets and other financial records. A manager or officer must research what other local banks are doing and how strong the economy is. These factors will influence what services the bank's customers will want. The bank officer usually prepares daily or weekly reports for the bank president.

The First ATM

In 1969, the country's first automatic teller machine was installed at Chemical Bank in Rockville Center, New York.

Bank clerks help to keep the vast amounts of paperwork and the computerized records in a bank in order. They keep track of deposit slips, checks, financial statements, and correspondence. They record transactions and file records. They may assist customers, answer telephone calls, and do other general duties.

A loan officer (right) explains loan options to a customer. (Bob Daemmrich, The Image Works)

EXPLORING

○ Visit these Web sites: Kids & Money (http://www.ext.nodak.edu/extnews/pipeline/d-parent.htm) and Investing For Kids (http://library.thinkquest.org/3096).

○ Read books and magazines about the banking industry and financial topics.

○ Volunteer to be the banker when you play games like Monopoly.

○ Ask your parents to teach you how to write checks and how to use a checkbook.

○ Ask your parents to help you open your own bank account.

Education and Training

Most banks prefer that bank clerks and bank tellers have at least a high school education. Employers look for applicants who have taken courses in bookkeeping, typing, business, and mathematics. You should also be able to operate business machines, including computers. Bank officers and managers need to understand finances, economics, and the rules and regulations of the banking industry. To become a bank officer or manager you will need a bachelor's degree in economics or business administration.

Earnings

Bank tellers earned average salaries of $22,140 a year in 2006, according to the U.S. Department of Labor. Clerks' salaries ranged from less than $19,760 to $46,020 or more per year. Bank officers and managers had starting salaries of $50,290. Experienced officers and managers earned $125,000 or more a year.

Outlook

Employment opportunities are expected to grow more slowly than the average for bank tellers because more people use automatic teller

The History of Banking

Banking in the United States began right after the Revolutionary War. The First Bank of the United States was a federal bank established to print money, purchase securities (stocks and bonds) in companies, and lend money. At the end of its 20-year charter, Congress refused to renew the First Bank's charter because of concern about the power that the bank held. The bank was soon closed. Another federal bank followed but only operated for four years before it suffered the same fate as the First Bank.

With the failures of the federal banks, state banks quickly grew in power and size. Each bank was allowed to issue its own currency, which created a huge variation in the number of dollars in existence. This affected the dollar's value. If the bank produced too much money, or lent money and did not receive enough of it back, the bank would close and depositors would lose everything they had invested.

In 1863, the National Bank Act was passed to charter state banks, issue national currency, and eventually tax the usage of bank currency. The taxation effectively killed all but the national currency. In 1913, Congress established the Federal Reserve. The Federal Reserve was started to act as the government's central bank. It was divided into 12 districts, with a board of governors to determine policy, supervise the fluctuation of currency reserves for banks, and print currency.

machines and online and telephone banking instead of tellers. However, the growing number of bank branches, together with longer hours and more services offered to attract more customers, will require more tellers. Employment for clerks and related workers is also predicted to grow more slowly than the average. Again, mergers, closings, and the use of computers and automated technologies have limited the number of new positions available. Average growth is predicted for bank officers and managers. They will be needed to help banks face greater competition, to handle changing tax laws, and to help banks comply with stricter record-keeping policies.

FOR MORE INFO

For information on money management for people of all ages, contact
American Bankers Association
1120 Connecticut Avenue NW
Washington, DC 20036
Tel: 800-226-5377
http://www.aba.com

For industry information, contact
Bank Administration Institute
One North Franklin, Suite 1000
Chicago, IL 60606-3421
E-mail: info@bai.org
http://www.bai.org

Bookkeepers

What Bookkeepers Do

Bookkeepers keep records of the finances of their companies. They may record these transactions in an account book or on a computer. From time to time, they prepare statements that summarize the funds received and paid out.

Bookkeeping records are very important to any company. They show how much money the company has and how much it owes. They also show how much money the company has earned or lost in a certain period of time. Bookkeeping records are especially important when a company submits income tax reports to the federal government and profit and loss reports to company owners.

Bookkeepers work for a wide variety of employers. These range from small businesses to large corporations. *General bookkeepers* usually work for small businesses. They may do all the tasks involved in keeping a complete set of bookkeeping records. They may also do other types of office work, such as filing papers and answering telephone calls or e-mails.

In large businesses, an accountant may supervise the workers in the bookkeeping department. These workers sometimes are called *accounting clerks*. They usually do specialized tasks. Some record items in account books and draft bills. Others prepare reports, write checks, or make payroll lists.

Key Bookkeeping Equipment

- fax machine
- copier
- computer with spreadsheet, word processing, and database software
- adding machine/calculator
- reference books, such as a yearly tax guide

EXPLORING

○ Keep an account of your own finances. Write down your income, including your allowance, gifts, or money you earn for odd jobs or babysitting. Write down your expenses—food and drink, clothing, music and movies, etc.

○ Volunteer to be the treasurer for school clubs.

○ Use your school's resource center or local library to find computer software designed for money management.

Bookkeepers need strong mathematical skills. They must be organized and able to concentrate on detailed work. The work is often tedious, and bookkeepers should not mind sitting for long hours behind a desk. They should be methodical, accurate, orderly, and enjoy working on detailed tasks. Employers look for honest, discreet, and trustworthy people, because they are placing their business in the bookkeeper's hands.

Education and Training

Bookkeepers must have at least a high school education. Employers prefer to hire those who have taken business courses in high school. Such courses include business, math, bookkeeping, and computers. Some employers look for people who have completed a junior college or business school training program. Others offer on-the-job training to workers.

Some schools and employers participate in work-study programs. In these programs, students work at part-time bookkeeping jobs. They also are required to attend class and complete class assignments.

Earnings

According to the U.S. Department of Labor, bookkeepers earned a median income of $30,560 a year in 2006. Earnings are also influenced by such factors as the size of the city where they work and the size and type of business by which

Where It All Began

The first known records of bookkeeping date back to 2600 B.C., when the Babylonians used pointed sticks to mark accounts on soft clay slabs. Around the same time, Middle Eastern and Egyptian cultures used a system of numbers to record merchants' trading of the grain and farm products that were distributed from storage warehouses.

Sometime after the start of the 13th century, the decimal numeration system was introduced in Europe, simplifying bookkeeping record systems. The merchants of Venice, Italy—one of the busiest trading centers in the world at that time—are credited with the invention of the double-entry bookkeeping method that is widely used today.

As industry in the United States grows more complex, simpler and quicker bookkeeping methods and procedures have evolved. Developments include bookkeeping machines, computer hardware and software, and electronic data processing.

they are employed. Clerks just starting out earned approximately $19,760 in 2006. Those with one or two years of college generally earn higher starting wages. Top-paying jobs averaged $46,020 or more in 2006.

A Career in Bookkeeping

What's the good news?
○ flexible hours
○ both part-time and full-time jobs are available
○ independent work conditions

What's the downside of bookkeeping jobs?
○ sometimes repetitive tasks
○ deadlines
○ government reporting

FOR MORE INFO

For information on certification and career opportunities, contact
American Institute of Professional Bookkeepers
6001 Montrose Road, Suite 500
Rockville, MD 20852-4873
Tel: 800-622-0121
E-mail: info@aipb.org
http://www.aipb.org

For more information on women in accounting, contact
The Educational Foundation for Women in Accounting
PO Box 1925
Southeastern, PA 19399-1925
Tel: 610-407-9229
E-mail: info@efwa.org
http://www.efwa.org

Outlook

More than two million people work in bookkeeping jobs. However, employment of bookkeepers and accounting clerks is expected to grow slowly in the next decade. Most job openings will be created as workers retire or change jobs. New jobs will become available as smaller businesses and industries expand. The use of computers makes the bookkeeper's job easier, but it also means that businesses need fewer bookkeepers to do the same amount of work.

Computer Systems Analysts

What Computer Systems Analysts Do

Computer systems analysts help banks, government offices, and businesses understand their computer systems. Most organizations now use computers to store data. They need analysts who can design computer systems and programs for the specific

Words to Learn

ASCII (American Standard Code for Information Exchange) numerical code used by personal computers

database a collection of information stored on a computer

debugging identifying and correcting errors in software

GUI (goo-ey; Graphical User Interface) a system that uses symbols (icons) seen onscreen to represent available functions

LAN (Local Area Network) a network that exists at one location, typically an office

network several computers that are electronically connected to share data and programs

spreadsheet a program that performs mathematical operations; used mainly for accounting and other record keeping

WAN (Wide Area Network) a network that includes remote sites in different buildings, cities, states, or countries

wireless network a telecommunications network that uses electromagnetic waves, rather than wires, to transmit information

EXPLORING

○ Surf the Internet regularly and read computer magazines.

○ Play strategy games, such as chess. Such games are a good way to use analytic thinking skills while having fun. The themes of commercial games range from war simulations to world historical development.

○ Learn everything you can about computers. Work and play with them on a daily basis.

○ Ask your teacher or guidance counselor to help you set up an information interview with a computer systems analyst.

○ You might want to try hooking up a mini-system at home or school, configuring terminals, printers, and modems. This activity requires a fair amount of knowledge and should be supervised by a professional.

needs of a business, or even to the needs of just one department in a business.

Computer systems analysts work with both the hardware and software parts of computer systems. Hardware includes the large items such as the computer itself, the monitor, and the keyboard. Software includes the computer programs, which are written and stored on disks, and the documentation (the manuals or guidebooks) that goes with the programs. Analysts design the best mix of hardware and software for the needs of the company that employs them.

A computer systems analyst for the personnel department of a large company, for example, would first talk to the department manager about which areas of the business could be helped by computer technology. If the company started a new policy of giving employees longer paid vacations at Christmas, the manager might want to know how this policy has affected company profits for the month of December. The analyst can show the manager what computer program to use, what data to enter, and how to read the charts or graphs that the computer produces. The work of the analyst allows the manager to review the raw data. The numbers show company profits as the same as or different from those in the previous

Decembers, and the manager can then make an informed decision about whether to continue the company policy.

Once analysts have the computer system set up and operating, they advise on equipment and programming changes. Often, people in a department each have their own computer, but they must be able to connect with and use information from each other's computers. Analysts must then work with all the different computers in a department or a company so the computers can connect with each other. This system of connected computers is called a network.

Education and Training

Take advanced high school classes in math, science, and computer science to prepare for this work. Since programmer analysts do a lot of proposal writing, it is a good idea to take English classes, too. Speech classes will help prepare you for making formal presentations to management and clients.

Where Do They Work?

Computer systems analysts work for all types of firms, including:

- ○ manufacturing companies
- ○ data processing service firms
- ○ hardware and software companies
- ○ banks
- ○ insurance companies
- ○ credit companies
- ○ publishing companies
- ○ government agencies
- ○ colleges and universities

Salaries in Information Technology

The following is a list of staff positions in the thriving IT industry and the corresponding average salaries:

Database Analyst	$62,747
E-Commerce Manager	$93,346
Information Security Specialist	$76,087
Network Administrator	$52,699
Programmer/Analyst	$65,030
Technology/Business Analyst	$68,579

Source: ComputerWorld, 2006

To be a computer systems analyst you will need at least a bachelor's degree in computer science. Analysts in specialized areas (aeronautics, for example) usually have graduate degrees as well. Also, training in mathematics, engineering, accounting, or business will be helpful in some cases.

In addition to a college degree, job experience as a computer programmer is very helpful. Many businesses choose computer programmers already on staff and train them on the job to be systems analysts. Computer systems analysts with several years of experience are often promoted into managerial jobs.

Earnings

Starting salaries for computer systems analysts average about $42,000 a year. After several years of experience, analysts can earn as much as $70,000 a year. Computer systems analysts with many years of experience and a master's degree can earn more than $106,000 a year. Salaries for analysts in government are somewhat lower than the average for private industry. Earnings also depend on years of experience and the type of business you work for.

Outlook

Employment for computer systems analysts will grow much faster than the average, according to the U.S. Department of Labor. Businesses are using more computers, and they will rely increasingly on systems analysts to make the right purchasing decisions and to keep systems running smoothly.

FOR MORE INFO

For information on career opportunities for women in computing, contact
Association for Women in Computing
41 Sutter Street, Suite 1006
San Francisco, CA 94104-4903
Tel: 415-905-4663
E-mail: info@awc-hq.org
http://www.awc-hq.org

For information on becoming an independent consultant, contact
Independent Computer Consultants Association
11131 South Towne Square, Suite F
St. Louis, MO 63123-7817
Tel: 800-774-4222
http://www.icca.org

For information on certification, contact
Institute for the Certification of Computing Professionals
2350 East Devon Avenue, Suite 115
Des Plaines, IL 60018-4610
Tel: 800-843-8227
E-mail: office@iccp.org
http://www.iccp.org

For information on careers in Information Technology, contact
National Workforce Center for Emerging Technologies
Bellevue Community College
3000 Landerholm Circle SE, N258
Bellevue, WA 98007-6484
http://www.nwcet.org/programs/cyberCareers/default.asp

Demographers

What Demographers Do

Demographers collect and study facts about a society's population—births, marriages, deaths, education, and income levels. Their population studies tell what the society is really like and help experts predict economic and social trends. For example, demographers may study the birth rates of a community. They may find that the population of school-age children is growing faster than expected and that new schools will have to be built. Or demographers may collect facts about how many of these children have been sick with measles. These facts could be studied to find out how effective the measles vaccine is.

Demographers work for both government agencies and private companies. Local, state, and federal government agencies use demographers to help them provide enough of the right kinds of transportation, education, police, and health services. Private companies need demographers' collections of facts, or statistics, to help them improve their products or services and predict who will buy them. For example, a retail chain might use a demographer's study to help decide the best location for a new store. Demographers may also teach in colleges and

Why Do We Need Population Statistics?

○ Population statistics, the basic tool of demography, include total population figures, population density (the average number of persons inhabiting each square mile), age, sex, and racial groupings, among other data.

○ Population statistics are used as the basis for assigning states' seats in the House of Representatives. For example, New York has more seats than Montana because there are more people per square mile. Accurate population statistics are necessary in planning immigration policies, public health programs, advertising and marketing campaigns, and other activities.

universities or work as consultants for private companies or communities as a whole.

Demographers use computers to help them gather and analyze the millions of pieces of information they need to make their forecasts. It is up to the individual demographer to know how to read the statistics and compile them in a meaningful way.

Education and Training

Students interested in this field should be good at solving logical problems and have strong skills in numbers and mathematics, especially algebra and geometry. In high school, you should take classes in social studies, English, and mathematics. Training in computer science is also helpful.

Demographers need a college degree in sociology or public health with special studies in demography. Many entry-level jobs require a master's degree.

As the field gets more competitive, many demographers (especially those who wish to work for the federal government) will earn a doctorate in sociology. The most successful demographers specialize in one area. You must also keep up with advances in the field by continuing your education throughout your career.

EXPLORING

○ Ask your mathematics teachers to give you some simple statistical problems related to population changes to practice the kinds of statistical techniques that demographers use.

○ Undertake your own demographic survey of an organization or group, such as your school or after-school club.

○ If you are in high school, try to get a part-time or summer job at a company with a statistical research department.

○ Talk with demographers about the rewards and demands of the field.

On the Web

Visit these Web sites to learn more about demography, statistics, and census information:

The CIA World Factbook
https://www.cia.gov/library/publications/the-world-factbook

FedStats
http://www.fedstats.gov

U.S. Census Bureau
http://www.census.gov

U.S. Stats

Here's an example of the kind of information demographers gather and use (estimates are from 2007 unless otherwise indicated):

Population: 301,139,947

Age structure:

0–14 years: 20.2 percent (male 31,152,050/female 29,777,438)

15–64 years: 67.2 percent (male 100,995,752/ female 101,365,035)

65 years and over: 12.6 percent (male 15,858,477/ female 21,991,195)

Birth rate: 14.16 births/1,000 population

Death rate: 8.26 deaths/1,000 population

Ethnic groups: white, 81.7 percent; black, 12.9 percent; Asian, 4.2 percent; Amerindian and Alaska Native, 1 percent; Native Hawaiian and other Pacific Islander, 0.2 percent (2003 est.)

Religions: Protestant, 52 percent; Roman Catholic, 24 percent; Mormon, 2 percent; Jewish, 1 percent; Muslim, 1 percent; other, 10 percent; none, 10 percent (2002 est.)

Languages: English, 82.1 percent; Spanish, 10.7 percent; other Indo-European, 3.8 percent; Asian and Pacific Island, 2.7 percent; other, 0.7 percent (2000 census)

Literacy: definition: age 15 and over can read and write total population: 99 percent (2003 est.)

Source: *CIA World Factbook*

Earnings

Earnings vary according to education, training, and place of employment. Salaries for social scientists (a group that includes demographers) ranged from less than $38,230 to more than $103,390 in 2006, according to the U.S.

Department of Labor. The median annual salary for social scientists was $64,920.

Outlook

There is a large amount of fact-gathering and social science research going on in the United States, and trained demographers will be needed to analyze this research. Job opportunities will be greatest in and around large cities, because that is where many colleges, universities, and other research facilities are located. There may be an increasing demand for demographers in international organizations such as the World Bank, the United Nations, and the World Health Organization. Demographers in these organizations will be needed to help developing countries analyze their own growing populations and plan for necessary services.

FOR MORE INFO

For career publications and education information, as well as job information, contact
American Sociological Association (ASA)
1307 New York Avenue NW, Suite 700
Washington, DC 20005-4701
Tel: 202-383-9005
E-mail: executive.office@asanet.org
http://www.asanet.org

Population Association of America
8630 Fenton Street, Suite 722
Silver Spring, MD 20910-3812
Tel: 301-565-6710
E-mail: info@popassoc.org
http://www.popassoc.org

For publications, special reports, and global population information, contact
Population Reference Bureau
1875 Connecticut Avenue NW,
    Suite 520
Washington, DC 20009-5728
Tel: 800-877-9881
E-mail: popref@prb.org
http://www.prb.org

For population statistics and information about the U.S. Census Bureau, contact
U.S. Census Bureau
4600 Silver Hill Road
Washington, DC 20233
Tel: 301-763-4748
http://www.census.gov

Engineering Technicians

What Engineering Technicians Do

You may not know it, but *engineering technicians* play a role in almost every part of our daily lives. You can thank engineering technicians (along with engineers, scientists, and other workers) for safer cars and planes, drugs that work effectively when you are sick, well-constructed buildings and highways, clean water and air, and the computer games you play for hours, among many other things that you might take for granted.

Engineering technicians use engineering, science, and mathematics to help engineers and other professionals in research and development, quality control, manufacturing, and many other fields. Some of the major specialties for technicians include chemical engineering, civil engineering, electrical and electronics engineering, industrial engineering, and mechanical engineering. The following paragraphs provide more information on these specialties:

Chemical engineering technicians assist chemists and chemical engineers in the research, development, testing, and manufacturing of chemicals and chemical-based products.

Civil engineering technicians help civil engineers design, plan, and build public as well as private works to meet a community's needs.

Electrical and electronics engineering technicians work individually or with engineers to help design, produce, improve, maintain, test, and repair a wide range of electronic equipment.

Industrial engineering technicians assist industrial engineers in their duties: they collect and analyze data and make recommendations for the efficient use of personnel, materials, and machines to produce goods or to provide services.

Mechanical engineering technicians work under the direction of mechanical engineers to design, build, maintain, and modify many kinds of machines, mechanical devices, and tools.

Engineering technicians work in a variety of conditions depending on their field of specialization. Technicians who specialize in design may find that they spend most of their time at the drafting board or computer. Those who specialize in manufacturing may work at a desk but also spend considerable time in manufacturing areas or shops.

Conditions also vary according to industry. Some industries require technicians to work in foundries, die-casting rooms, machine shops, assembly areas, or punch-press areas. Most of these areas, however, are well lighted, heated, and ventilated. Moreover, most industries employing mechanical engineering technicians have strong safety programs.

Education and Training

In high school, take algebra, geometry, science, trigonometry, calculus, chemistry, mechanical drawing, shop, and physics. Because computers have become essential for engineering technicians, computer courses are also important. Additionally, English and speech courses will help you improve your verbal and written communication skills.

EXPLORING

○ Read books and magazines about engineering and careers in engineering technology.
○ Visit the Junior Engineering Technical Society's Web site (http://www.jets.org) for information on engineering careers, competitions, and programs.
○ Join science and math clubs at your school.
○ Work on science projects that involve inventing and building. Enter a project in a science fair.
○ Try to visit a variety of different kinds of engineering facilities: service shops, manufacturing plants, and research laboratories. These visits will give you a realistic idea of the opportunities in the different areas of the industry.
○ Talk to engineering technicians about their careers. Ask them questions. What do they like and dislike about their jobs? Do they travel for their work? What type of education did they have to complete to prepare for the field? What is the employment outlook for their specialty?

Other Specialties

○ *Aeronautical and aerospace engineering technicians* design, construct, test, operate, and maintain the basic structures of aircraft and spacecraft, as well as propulsion and control systems.

○ *Biomedical engineering technicians* use engineering and life science principles to help biomedical engineers and scientists research biological aspects of animal and human life.

○ *Environmental engineering technicians* help environmental engineers and scientists design, build, and maintain systems to control waste streams produced by municipalities or private industry. Environmental engineering technicians typically focus on one of three areas: air, land, or water.

○ *Materials engineering technicians* work in support of materials engineers and scientists. These jobs involve the production, quality control, and experimental study of metals, ceramics, glass, plastics, semiconductors, and composites (combinations of these materials).

○ *Petroleum engineering technicians* help petroleum engineers and scientists improve petroleum drilling technology, maximize field production, and provide technical assistance.

○ *Robotics technicians* assist robotics engineers in a wide variety of tasks relating to the design, development, production, testing, operation, repair, and maintenance of robots and robotic devices.

While some current engineering technicians enter the field without formal academic training, it is increasingly difficult to do so. Most employers are interested in hiring graduates with at least a two-year degree in engineering technology. Technical institutes, community colleges, vocational schools, and universities all offer this course of study.

Some engineering technicians decide to pursue advancement in their field by becoming engineer technologists. Others decide to branch off into research and development or become engineers. These higher-level and higher-paid positions typically require the completion of a bachelor's degree in engineering technology (for engineering technologists) or at least a bachelor's degree in engineering (for technicians interested in engineering and in research and development).

An engineering technician reviews blueprints at a manufacturing plant. (National Renewable Energy Laboratory)

Earnings

The earnings of engineering technicians vary widely depending on skills and experience, the type of work, geographical

Mean Annual Earnings for Selected Engineering Technician Specialties, 2006

Aerospace Engineering and Operations Technicians	$54,480
Civil Engineering Technicians	$42,380
Electrical and Electronics Engineering Technicians	$50,840
Environmental Engineering Technicians	$43,100
Industrial Engineering Technicians	$50,920
Mechanical Engineering Technicians	$47,710

Source: U.S. Department of Labor

FOR MORE INFO

For more information on careers in engineering and engineering technology, contact

American Society for Engineering Education
1818 N Street NW, Suite 600
Washington, DC 20036-2479
Tel: 202-331-3500
http://www.asee.org

For industry information, contact
American Society of Certified Engineering Technicians
PO Box 1536
Brandon, MS 39043-1536
Tel: 601-824-8991
http://www.ascet.org

Junior Engineering Technical Society (JETS)
1420 King Street, Suite 405
Alexandria, VA 22314-2750
Tel: 703-548-5387
E-mail: info@jets.org
http://www.jets.org

location, and other factors. Salaries range from less than $25,000 to $79,000 or more annually.

Outlook

Employment of engineering technicians is expected to increase about as fast as the average, according to the U.S. Department of Labor. Computer-aided design allows individual technicians to increase productivity, which limits job growth. Technicians with training in sophisticated technologies and those with degrees in technology will have the best employment opportunities.

Engineers

What Engineers Do

Engineers, more than any other professionals, are responsible for discoveries and inventions that are part of our everyday lives. They use scientific knowledge and tools to design products, structures, and machines. Most engineers specialize in a particular area. *Electrical and electronics engineers,* for example, work in the medical, computer, missile guidance, and power distribution fields. Engineers have a wide range of choices in the type of work they can do. Almost every industry uses some type of engineer.

A nuclear power station is a good example of how different engineering specialties work together. *Civil engineers* help

Engineering Specialties

- aerospace and aeronautical engineers
- air quality engineers
- architectural engineers
- automotive engineers
- biomedical engineers
- chemical engineers
- civil engineers
- electrical engineers
- environmental engineers
- fiber optics engineers
- hardware engineers
- health and safety engineers
- industrial engineers
- mechanical engineers
- mining engineers
- nuclear engineers
- optical engineers
- petroleum engineers
- pollution control engineers
- quality control engineers
- robotics engineers
- software engineers

select the site for the power station. They draw blueprints for all structural details of the building. *Nuclear engineers* handle every stage of the production of nuclear energy, from processing nuclear fuels to disposing of radioactive wastes. *Environmental engineers* also find ways to safely dispose of such wastes. *Mechanical engineers* design and build engines that use nuclear fuel to produce power. *Electrical engineers* design equipment to distribute the electricity to thousands of customers. The device workers wear to detect the levels of radiation their bodies absorb over a period of time was developed by *biomedical engineers*.

There are 1.4 million engineers in the United States. All engineers, whatever their specialty, have a strong math and science background and an ability to develop solutions to practical problems. All engineers are problem solvers and inventors. They all do highly technical work. They must have a thorough knowledge of how the world works, from electronics to the human body, in order to come up with better ways of doing things.

Education and Training

Take a great deal of mathematics in high school, including geometry, trigonometry, calculus, and two years of algebra. You should also develop a strong background in physics, chemistry, biology, and computer programming or applications. Because engineers must communicate constantly with other engineers, scientists, clients, and consumers, four years of language arts is essential.

Engineers all have at least a four-year college degree that gives them a clear understanding of how math and science applies to the everyday world. Most engineering degrees are in electrical, mechanical, or civil engineering. Graduates of these programs may then choose to further specialize in their area of

Mean Annual Earnings for Selected Engineering Specialties, 2006

Aerospace Engineers	$89,260
Agricultural Engineers	$67,810
Biomedical Engineers	$78,030
Chemical Engineers	$81,600
Civil Engineers	$72,120
Electrical Engineers	$78,900
Electronics Engineers	$82,820
Environmental Engineers	$72,590
Hardware Engineers	$91,280
Health and Safety Engineers	$68,400
Industrial Engineers	$70,630
Marine Engineers	$75,400
Materials Engineers	$75,960
Mechanical Engineers	$72,580
Mining/Geological Engineers	$77,620
Nuclear Engineers	$92,040
Petroleum Engineers	$101,620

Source: U.S. Department of Labor

interest by taking more college courses or getting on-the-job training. For example, a mechanical engineer who wants to work with nuclear reactors may study nuclear science beyond the undergraduate level or may take an entry-level engineering job at a nuclear plant before working up to becoming an actual nuclear engineer.

Earnings

Engineers are paid well for their work. Their salaries are among the highest starting salaries of any career. According to the National Association of Colleges and Employers, new

FOR MORE INFO

For more information on careers in engineering, contact
American Society for Engineering Education
1818 N Street NW, Suite 600
Washington, DC 20036-2479
Tel: 202-331-3500
http://www.asee.org

For information on engineering careers and student clubs and competitions, contact
Junior Engineering Technical Society
1420 King Street, Suite 405
Alexandria, VA 22314-2750
Tel: 703-548-5387
E-mail: info@jets.org
http://www.jets.org

For information on licensure and practice areas, contact
National Society of Professional Engineers
1420 King Street
Alexandria, VA 22314-2794
Tel: 703-684-2800
http://www.nspe.org

The following Web site offers a variety of useful resources to inspire young women to pursue careers in engineering
Engineer Girl!
http://www.engineergirl.org

Visit the following Web site to purchase an inexpensive, comprehensive guide on careers in engineering
Engineering: Go For It!
http://www.engineering-goforit.com

engineers with bachelor's degrees averaged $43,000 to $61,000 a year in 2005 depending on their specialty. Those with master's degrees and no experience averaged $48,000 to $64,000 a year. Engineers with several years of experience and education can earn $100,000 or more a year.

Outlook

Engineers have great job security. Their work is necessary for keeping and improving our way of life. Even when the economy is not healthy, engineers' jobs are generally safe. Demand will continue to be strong for engineers with a solid math and science background and training in new technologies.

A chemical engineer conducts an experiment. (Keith Weller, USDA, Agricultural Research Service)

Financial Planners

What Financial Planners Do

Financial planners advise their clients on many aspects of finance. They do not work alone. Financial planners meet with their clients' other advisors, such as attorneys, accountants, trust officers, and investment bankers. This helps financial planners understand everything about their clients' overall finances. After meeting with the clients and their other advisors, financial planners analyze the information and write a report. This report lists the clients' financial objectives, current income, investments, expenses, tax returns, insurance, retirement programs, estate plans, and other important information. The report also includes recommendations on how the clients can best achieve their financial goals.

Financial planning is an ongoing process. The plan must be reviewed often so that changes can be made, if necessary, to make sure that it continues to meet the client's needs.

Words to Learn

assets   resources that have money value, including cash, inventory, real estate, machinery, collectibles, and securities; current assets are those that can be converted to cash within a year, while fixed assets are long-term assets, such as buildings, pieces of land, or patents that will not be converted to cash within a year

liabilities   debts or money owed; current liabilities are debts that must be paid within a year

net income   profit after taxes

net worth   value found by subtracting all liabilities from all assets

Since they handle all of the money and investments that people have worked a lifetime to earn, financial planners must be ready to answer difficult questions about the plans they write.

People need financial planners for different reasons. Some might want life insurance, college savings plans, or estate planning. Sometimes these needs are caused by changes in people's lives, such as retirement, death of a spouse, disability, marriage, birth of children, or job changes. Financial planners spend most of their time on investment planning, retirement planning, tax planning, estate planning, and risk management. All of these areas require different types of financial knowledge.

For example, financial planners who are *retirement counselors* look at whether the client will be happy with simple living, or want to travel the world first class. Other issues must be addressed, such as relocation costs (the amount of money it will take to move to another city, perhaps in a warmer climate), if any, or medical insurance needs. They must know about traditional sources of retirement funds, such as Social Security, personal savings, employer-sponsored plans, post-retirement employment, and inheritance (the passing on of money or property after an individual dies). Another retirement issue is the possibility of disability and the need for chronic illness care. Retirement planners may suggest disability income insurance, long-term care insurance, or a medical savings account as a precaution for such situations.

EXPLORING

○ Check out the financial planning information available on the Internet to familiarize yourself with the terms used in the industry. Visit these Web sites: Investing for Kids (http://library.thinkquest. org/3096), United States Mint H.I.P. Pocket Change (http://www. usmint.gov/kids), and YoungInvestor.com (http://www.younginvestor.com).

○ Take as many finance and business classes as possible.

○ If you live near a stock exchange, go for a visit. Most exchanges have their own Web sites.

○ Talk to certified financial planners to learn more about the career.

Planners must also know about asset management, employee benefits, insurance, and investments.

Financial planners must deal well with people, since it is important to maintain good relationships with clients.

Financial planners use various ways to find new clients, such as making telephone calls and giving seminars on financial planning.

Education and Training

In high school, you should take math classes and as many business classes as possible. Communications courses, such as speech or acting, will help put you at ease with talking in front of a crowd. English courses will help you prepare written reports.

Most financial planners earn a bachelor's degree in business or science. You could earn a business administration degree with a specialty in financial planning. You could also earn a liberal arts degree with courses in accounting, business administration, economics, finance, marketing, human behavior, counseling, and public speaking.

It's a Fact

- The first American colonists used English, French, and Spanish money. In 1775, just before the Revolutionary War, the Continental Congress issued money to finance the war. Paul Revere made the first plates for this currency.

- The 1792 Mint Act established the coin system, with the dollar as the main unit.

- The United States became the first country in the world to use the decimal system for currency.

- The first coins were made in 1793 at the Philadelphia Mint.

- The first paper money issued by the government was "demand notes," nicknamed "greenbacks."

Earnings

The U.S. Department of Labor reports that financial planners earned median annual salaries of $66,120 in 2006. The most-experienced financial planners with the highest level of education earned more than $114,260, while the least-experienced financial planners earned less than $32,340.

Financial planners must have good communication skills in order to interact successfully with clients. (Paul Barton, Corbis)

Outlook

Employment of financial planners is expected to grow rapidly in the future. When the economy is good people earn more and inherit more. This means they will have more money to invest. More and more people will need advice from financial planners about the many investment choices available.

FOR MORE INFO

For information on financial planning and certification, contact
Certified Financial Planner Board of Standards
1670 Broadway, Suite 600
Denver, CO 80202-4809
Tel: 888-237-6275
http://www.cfp.net

For information on financial planning, visit the FPA's Web site
Financial Planning Association (FPA)
4100 East Mississippi Avenue, Suite 400
Denver, CO 80246-3053
Tel: 800-322-4237
http://www.fpanet.org

For more information on fee-only financial advisors, contact
National Association of Personal Financial Advisors
3250 North Arlington Heights Road, Suite 109
Arlington Heights, IL 60004-1574
Tel: 800-366-2732
E-mail: info@napfa.org
http://www.napfa.org

Geophysicists

What Geophysicists Do

Geophysicists study the physical structure of the Earth. This includes land surfaces, underground areas, and bodies of water. They use their knowledge to predict earthquakes, discover oil, and find places to build power plants. Their duties may include fieldwork, laboratory research, or college teaching.

Geophysics combines the sciences of geology and physics. Geophysicists usually specialize in one area of geophysics. For example, *seismologists* study earthquakes. *Hydrologists* study the movement and distribution of water. *Meteorologists* study weather patterns. No matter what their area of specialization, geophysicists use the scientific principles of geology, chemistry, mathematics, physics, and engineering. Many of their instruments, such as the seismograph, take precise measurements of the earth's physical characteristics, such as its electric, magnetic, and gravitational fields. *Field geophysicists* work outdoors in all kinds of weather. They often travel and work in isolated areas.

Other Types of Geophysicists

Geodesists measure the shape and size of the Earth to determine fixed points, positions, and elevations on or near the Earth's surface.

Geomagnetists use specialized equipment to measure variations in the Earth's magnetic field from magnetic observatories and stations.

Applied geophysicists use data gathered from the air and ground, as well as computers, to analyze the Earth's crust. They look for oil and mineral deposits and try to find places that can be used to safely dispose of hazardous wastes.

Exploration geophysicists, sometimes called **geophysical prospectors**, use seismic techniques to look for possible oil and gas deposits.

Volcanologists study volcanoes, their location, and their activity.

Planetologists study the makeup and atmosphere of the planets, the Moon, and other bodies in our solar system.

Geophysicists often study environmental issues. For example, they may investigate whether an explosion designed to expose rich mineral deposits might also lead to an earthquake. They might examine the quality of underground water and how it affects a city's drinking supply.

Education and Training

Geophysicists should have a solid background in mathematics and the physical and earth sciences. In high school you should take four years of mathematics and courses in earth science, physics, and chemistry. Classes in mechanical drawing, history, and English are also highly recommended.

The best way to become a geophysicist is to get a bachelor's degree in geophysics or geology. A degree in physics, mathematics, or chemistry might be sufficient, but you should also take as many geology courses as you can. You will need a master's degree or doctorate in geology or geophysics for research positions, college teaching jobs, and other opportunities with good advancement potential.

Earnings

According to the U.S. Department of Labor, geoscientists (which includes geologists, geophysicists, and oceanographers) earned an average annual

EXPLORING

○ You can find out more about geophysics by reading books on rocks and minerals, metals and metallurgy, the universe and space, and weather and climate.
○ Develop hobbies that deal with radio, electronics, rock collecting, or map collecting.
○ Visit the Society of Exploration Geophysicists kids' Web site at http://students.seg.org/kids.
○ Talk to a geophysicist about his or her career.

Volcanologists collect soil samples from within Mount Pinatubo in the Philippines. (Roger Ressmeyer, Corbis)

Earth-Shattering Facts

○ Scientists believe that the San Andreas Fault may be 100 million years old. It cuts through the state of California for almost 1,800 miles. Small earthquakes along the San Andreas Fault occur several times a month. Not all earthquakes are dangerous, but many lives have been lost due to earthquakes along the fault. In the 1906 San Francisco earthquake, 1,300 people died from falling buildings and fires. The city burned for three days.

○ There are over a million quakes around the world each year, including those too small to be felt.

○ An earthquake occurs once every 30 seconds.

○ The largest number of people killed in an earthquake is approximately 830,000 (in China in 1556).

○ The great Alaska earthquake of March 27, 1964, was the strongest earthquake in the United States. It had a magnitude of 9.2. Approximately 125 people died, with most of the deaths due to the tsunami (seismic wave) it generated. Shaking was felt for an estimated seven minutes, and raised or lowered the ground surface as much as 150 feet in some areas.

○ An earthquake with a magnitude 9.5 that took place in Chile in 1960 was the largest known earthquake and resulted in around 6,000 deaths. It triggered a tsunami that killed people as far away as Hawaii and Japan.

○ Alaska has more earthquakes per year than the combined total of the rest of the United States. As many as 4,000 are recorded there every year.

Source: Center for Earthquake Research and Information

salary of $72,660 in 2006. Salaries ranged from less than $39,740 to more than $135,950 annually. In 2006, the average salary for a geophysicist working for the federal government was $86,240.

Outlook

Many geophysicists explore for oil and gas. Their employment opportunities depend on the strength of the petroleum industry. But even if job prospects in the oil industry are not good, there will continue to be jobs in teaching and other research areas.

FOR MORE INFO

For information on geoscience careers, contact
American Geological Institute
4220 King Street
Alexandria, VA 22302-1502
Tel: 703-379-2480
http://www.agiweb.org

For industry information, contact
American Geophysical Union
2000 Florida Avenue NW
Washington, DC 20009-1277
Tel: 800-966-2481
http://www.agu.org

For career information and profiles of women in geophysics, visit the AWG's Web site
Association for Women Geoscientists (AWG)
PO Box 30645

Lincoln, NE 68503-0645
E-mail: office@awg.org
http://www.awg.org

For information on careers in geophysics, contact
Society of Exploration Geophysicists
PO Box 702740
Tulsa, OK 74170-2740
Tel: 918-497-5500
http://www.seg.org

For information on the geosciences and to read the online publication, "Become a Geophysicist... A What?" visit the following Web sites
U.S. Geological Survey
http://www.usgs.gov/education
http://earthquake.usgs.gov/learning/kids/become.php

Math Teachers

What Math Teachers Do

Math teachers help students learn simple and advanced math theories and apply these concepts to everyday life. They work in elementary, middle school, and high school classrooms. Some math teachers may also work as adult education teachers. Professors usually teach at the college level.

Math teachers teach complex mathematical subjects such as algebra, calculus, geometry, trigonometry, and statistics to middle and high school students. They may teach algebra to a class of ninth graders one period and trigonometry to high school seniors the next. Teachers must be able to get along with young people, have patience, and like to help others. They need good communication skills, since they often work

Profile: Grace Hopper (1906–1992)

When mathematician Grace Hopper was young, her hobbies were needlepoint, reading, and playing the piano. Her father encouraged her to pursue things that interested her, even if they were considered more "masculine" pursuits. In 1943, she was sworn into the U.S. Navy Reserve, where she served for 43 years.

Hopper coined the term "bug," meaning a computer fault, while working on the Harvard Mark II computer. The real bug in the Mark II was a moth that caused a hardware problem.

In 1969, the Data Processing Management Association named her the first computer science "Man of the Year," and she was awarded the National Medal of Technology in 1991.

with students from varying ethnic backgrounds and cultures.

Math teachers teach specific subjects, but they must also make learning fun and teach students how to work together. Some schools use less structured classrooms to teach math skills, team problem solving, and cooperation. Math teachers encourage creative and logical thinking as it relates to math and education in general. They often use various teaching methods to keep students interested and help them learn. They may use games, computers, and experiments as hands-on teaching tools in the classroom. They may schedule field trips, guest speakers, or special events to show students how math skills are used in their daily lives and in the operation of businesses and government.

Math teachers also develop lesson plans, create exams, correct papers, calculate grades, and keep records. Some schools may also require teachers to lead extracurricular activities such as math club, competitions, and events. Teachers meet with and advise students, hold parent-teacher conferences, and attend faculty meetings. In addition, they may have to attend local, state, and national conferences. Teachers must take continuing education courses to maintain their state's teaching license.

EXPLORING

- By attending your own math classes, you've already gained a good sense of the daily work of a math teacher. But teachers have many duties beyond the classroom, so ask to spend some time with one of your teachers after school. Ask about their job and how they prepared for their career, and look at lecture notes and record-keeping procedures.
- Teach a younger sister or brother to count or do basic arithmetic, such as addition and subtraction. As they get a little older, you can teach them the value of coins and how to make change.
- Your school or community may have a volunteer program where you can tutor younger children in math.

Education and Training

If you want to pursue a career as a math teacher, you should take high school math courses including algebra, geometry,

A math teacher discusses a math problem with a student. (Sven Martson, The Image Works)

trigonometry, and calculus. More advanced classes in probability, statistics, and logic are also beneficial if they are available. Computer science, psychology, and English classes are also recommended.

There are more than 500 accredited teacher education programs in the United States. Most of these programs are designed to meet the certification requirements for the state in which they're located. Some states may require that you pass a test before being admitted to an education program. You may choose to major in mathematics while taking required education courses, or you may major in secondary education with a concentration in math. Although requirements for teaching licenses vary by state, all public schools require teachers to

Math is Everywhere

We use math every day in all kinds of ways. Here are some examples:

○ Art. Artists use triangles, squares, rectangles, circles, and other geometric shapes. Some artists use math when they create special formulas to mix their own paints, chemicals, or other materials.

○ Music. Rhythm is based on counting. Think of whole notes, half notes, quarter notes, and eighth notes and you are thinking in fractions.

○ Sports. Math is used in sports for scoring, figuring averages and percentages, and compiling statistics.

○ Health. Temperature, heart rate, pulse, and blood pressure all are measured in numbers. Diet and nutrition use basic math to figure calories, fat grams, and recommended daily allowances. You use math to figure dosages for drugs.

have a bachelor's degree and complete the state's approved training program.

Earnings

According to the U.S. Department of Labor, the median annual salary for secondary school teachers was $47,740 in 2006. Salaries ranged from less than $31,760 to $76,100 or more annually. The median annual salary of middle school teachers was

Think About It

How do people in these jobs use math every day?

- carpentry
- cooking
- farming
- graphic design
- photography
- publishing
- real estate
- sales
- sewing

FOR MORE INFO

For more information on a teaching career, contact

American Federation of Teachers
555 New Jersey Avenue NW
Washington, DC 20001-2079
Tel: 202-879-4400
E-mail: online@aft.org
http://www.aft.org

For information on careers in mathematics, contact

American Mathematical Society
201 Charles Street
Providence, RI 02904-2294
Tel: 800-321-4AMS
E-mail: ams@ams.org
http://www.ams.org

For information on competitions for high school students, contact

The Mathematical Association of America

1529 18th Street NW
Washington, DC 20036-1358
Tel: 800-741-9415
http://www.maa.org/students/middle_high

For information on teaching careers in mathematics, contact

National Council of Teachers of Mathematics
1906 Association Drive
Reston, VA 20191-1502
Tel: 703-620-9840
http://www.nctm.org

For information on public education, contact

National Education Association
1201 16th Street NW
Washington, DC 20036-3290
Tel: 202-833-4000
http://www.nea.org

$46,300 in 2006. The lowest paid 10 percent of these teachers earned less than $31,450, and the top 10 percent made $73,350 or more per year. College math teachers earned $56,420 a year in 2006.

Outlook

Teachers are generally in short supply across the nation due to rising school enrollments and the number of teachers who are retiring. Math teachers are particularly needed. According to surveys conducted by the American Federation of Teachers, school districts report a considerable shortage of math teachers, with greater shortages occurring in large cities.

Operations Research Analysts

What Operations Research Analysts Do

Operations research analysts are help companies work more smoothly and with less waste of time and money. The job duties of analysts vary depending on their employers, but all follow the same general steps in doing their work. First, company managers describe a business problem to the analyst. For example, a bank president might want to improve ways to process checks.

Analysts then make mathematical models of how checks are currently processed. To do this, they divide the present system into steps. They give a number value to each step. Then analysts study the mathematical relationships between the steps. The model can be changed to figure out what will happen to the system under different conditions. Many models are computerized. Thus, analysts need to be able to use or write computer programs.

Operations research analysts can work for a variety of employers. These include manufacturers of machinery and transportation equipment, banks, telecommunications companies, insurance companies, and management consultants.

Where Do They Work?

Major employers of operations research analysts include:
- computer systems design firms
- telecommunications companies
- insurance companies
- banks and other financial institutions
- private management consulting firms
- the federal government, especially the armed forces and the U.S. Department of Defense
- state and local government

EXPLORING

- Because this field requires advanced study, it is hard to get hands-on experience while in school. However, if you are in high school, you can try to get a part-time job at a bank or insurance company with an in-house operations research department to give you some exposure to the career.
- Consider enrolling in special summer sessions or advanced placement mathematics courses to further develop your knowledge of mathematics.

The federal government, especially the armed forces, also hires analysts.

Operations research analysts often work as part of a research team consisting of other mathematicians and engineers, and they frequently use data processing equipment in their research. They prepare written and oral reports of their findings for upper-management officials.

Education and Training

School courses that can help you prepare for this career include mathematics, English composition, and computer science.

Some employers want analysts to have a bachelor's degree in mathematics, business administration, or operations research. Others expect

Let's Get Technical

- Operations research analysts use *queuing theory* to study the flow of people or goods. Walt Disney World uses queuing theory to keep the lines moving at Space Mountain.
- An operations research analyst uses *stochastic (random, chance) modeling* to predict the number and kind of personnel a company will need over a five-year period. It is also used to schedule routes for airlines.
- *Optimization* is used to find the best way to meet certain requirements. For example, it helps determine how timber should be cut to minimize waste and maximize profits.

Source: Institute for Operations Research and the Management Sciences

employees to have master's degrees in one of these fields. More employers are looking for analysts with degrees in computer science, information science, or data processing. Analysts who work for the government usually have to pass a civil service examination. New employees usually get several months of on-the-job training.

Earnings

According to the U.S. Department of Labor, the median annual salary of operations research analysts was $64,650 in 2006. Salaries ranged from less than $38,760 to $108,290 or more. Operations research analysts who work for the federal government usually earn higher salaries than those in private companies.

FOR MORE INFO

For more information about a career as an operations research analyst, contact

Institute for Operations Research and the Management Sciences
7240 Parkway Drive, Suite 310
Hanover, MD 21076-1310
Tel: 800-446-3676
E-mail: informs@informs.org
http://www.informs.org

Society for Industrial and Applied Mathematics
3600 University City Science Center
Philadelphia, PA 19104-2688
Tel: 215-382-9800
http://www.siam.org

Outlook

According to the U.S. Department of Labor, growth within the field of operations research is predicted to be slower than the average. Despite slow growth, opportunities in operations research should still be good. During slower and hence more competitive economic periods, analysts are needed to help companies increase their productivity or lower operating costs.

Optical Engineers

What Optical Engineers Do

Optics is the study of light and how it interacts with matter. It is a branch of physics and engineering. *Optical engineers* use their knowledge of how light is produced, sent, detected, and measured to design such things as wireless communications, audio/CD/DVD players, high-definition television, laser printers, atomic research, robotics, and medical and scientific methods and tools.

Optical engineers may design optical systems for cameras, telescopes, or lens systems. They fine-tune optical devices. They design and develop circuitry and parts for devices that use optical technology. These engineers may also design and test instruments that measure how well optical systems are working.

To create a new product using optical technology, optical engineers follow a many-step process. They study the problem to understand it thoroughly. Then they use their imagination and training to come up with a solution for the problem. Once they have an idea, they turn it into a design or several designs. They use a computer to create a model, or they make a sample. They test the model or sample and change

Options for Optics Engineers

Optics is a growing field. Optical engineers today work in these areas:

- image processing
- information processing
- wireless communications
- audio/CD/DVD technology
- high-definition television
- laser printers
- astronomical observation
- atomic research
- robotics
- military surveillance
- water-quality monitoring
- undersea monitoring
- medical and scientific procedures and instruments

it as they find problems. They repeat this building and testing until they feel that their product is complete. The design is then sent to a company that manufactures it. Optical engineers often work with a team of engineers, industrial designers, technologists, and technicians.

Some optical engineers specialize in lasers and fiber optics. They are known as *fiber optics engineers* and *laser and fiber optics engineers*. Fiber optics are thin, hair-like strands of plastic-coated glass fibers that transmit light and images. Lasers may be used to generate the light in these fibers. Lasers are devices that produce thin, powerful beams of light. They can be used in medical and surgical procedures, manufacturing, robotics, printing, and military systems, such as navigation systems and weapons systems. Fiber optics technology is used in sensors that detect temperature, pressure, and other physical features. This technology is also used in communications systems such as telephone systems, computer networks, and fiber optic imaging (which involves the use of fiber optics to transmit light or images).

EXPLORING

○ Your teacher or librarian can help you find books and videos on optics.

○ Join science and engineering clubs that offer opportunities for experimentation, problem solving, and team-building activities.

○ Ask your teacher or a parent to help you perform simple experiments that examine the properties of light. Books on optics often provide instructions for experiments.

Education and Training

In high school, take physical science, physics, chemistry, geometry, algebra, trigonometry, calculus, social studies, English, composition, and computer science classes. Courses in computer-aided design will also be helpful.

You must have a bachelor's degree in engineering to become an optical engineer. Many colleges offer classes in optics. Only a very small number of schools, though, offer

Scientists See the Light

The study of the properties of light began during the 1600s when Galileo built telescopes to observe the planets and stars. Scientists, such as Sir Isaac Newton, conducted experiments and studies that contributed to the understanding of light and how it operates. Among Newton's many experiments was his work with prisms to break sunlight into a spectrum of colors. Christiaan Huygens, a Dutch physicist, also performed important studies and developed a theory about the wave properties of light.

degree programs in optical engineering. Most colleges offer degrees in a related field, such as electrical engineering or physics, with a specialization in optics. Most programs take four or five years to complete. Some colleges require internships or cooperative work programs during which you work at a related job for one to three semesters.

Many students receive master's degrees. Those who plan to work in research usually earn a doctoral degree.

Earnings

Entry-level optical engineers earn about $49,000 a year. Those engineers with 10 years of experience average about $75,000 a year and even more. The highest-paid optical engineers earn more than $115,000.

Outlook

Opportunities for optical engineers will be very good in the next decade. New uses for optics technology are discovered all the time. The use of fiber optics technology in telecommunications is increasing, which will lead to more opportunities for engineers in the computer, broadcasting, cable, and telephone industries. Optical engineers will also find jobs in the medical and defense fields.

FOR MORE INFO

For information on engineering careers and student clubs and competitions, contact
Junior Engineering Technical Society
1420 King Street, Suite 405
Alexandria, VA 22314-2750
Tel: 703-548-5387
E-mail: info@jets.org
http://www.jets.org

For information on careers, contact the following organizations
Lasers and Electro-Optics Society
c/o The Institute of Electrical and Electronics Engineers
445 Hoes Lane
Piscataway, NJ 08854-4141
Tel: 732 562-3891
E-mail: soc.leo@ieee.org
http://www.i-leos.org

Optical Society of America
2010 Massachusetts Avenue NW
Washington, DC 20036-1012
Tel: 202-223-8130
E-mail: info@osa.org
http://www.osa.org

For information on colleges, scholarships, and student membership, and to participate in an online student forum, visit the SPIE's Web site
SPIE—The International Society for Optical Engineering
PO Box 10
Bellingham, WA 98227-0010
Tel: 888-504-8171
E-mail: spie@spie.org
http://www.spie.org

For information on optics and careers in the field, visit
Optics For Teens
http://www.opticsforteens.org

Physicists

What Physicists Do

Physicists try to understand the laws of nature and learn how to use these laws in practical ways. Some teach in high schools and colleges, some work for the federal government, and some work for industrial laboratories. Wherever they work, physicists spend a great deal of time doing research, performing laboratory experiments, and studying the results.

Physicists are concerned with the special properties of matter and energy. *Theoretical physicists* try to understand how matter and energy work. *Experimental physicists* perform experiments that test exactly what various kinds of matter and energy do. Then they try to come up with practical ways to use them.

Physicists work in many areas. Some study atoms to learn the secrets of nuclear energy. Others work with engineers to find the best ways to build bridges and dams. Others conduct experiments for petroleum companies to find better ways to obtain, refine, and use crude oil. Physicists are important to the space program. They try to figure out what outer space is actually like, and they design and test spaceships. Physicists often work with other scientists, such as chemists, biologists, and geologists. Biophysics and geophysics are two fields of science that were

Famous Physics Labs

Brookhaven National Laboratory (http://www.bnl.gov/world) in Upton, Long Island, New York, is mainly involved in studies of nuclear physics.

Fermi National Accelerator Laboratory (http://www.fnal.gov) in Batavia, Illinois, conducts research in high-energy physics.

Lawrence Berkeley National Laboratory (http://www.lbl.gov) in Berkeley, California, conducts research in fundamental studies of the universe, quantitative biology, nanoscience, new energy systems and environmental solutions, and integrated computing.

Los Alamos National Laboratory (http://www.lanl.gov) in Los Alamos, New Mexico, conducts research in nuclear weapons and energy, cryogenic physics, space sciences, molecular biology, and metallurgy.

created when these scientists began to work together.

Physicists may specialize in mechanics, heat, optics (light), acoustics (sound), electricity and magnetism, electronics, particle physics (atoms and molecules), nuclear physics, or physics of fluids.

Education and Training

In high school, take as many mathematics courses and science as your school offers. English skills are important, as you must write up your results, communicate with other scientists. In addition, get as much experience as possible working with computers.

There are some jobs available for physicists with only a bachelor's degree from a four-year college. If you have a bachelor's degree, you may be able to find a basic research job. If you have a teaching certificate, you can teach in secondary school.

Most physicists will need to go on for further education if they want to advance in the field. The more challenging and rewarding jobs go to physicists who have master's degrees and doctorates.

Earnings

According to the U.S. Department of Labor, the median salary for physicists was $94,240 in 2006. Salaries ranged

EXPLORING

○ Ask your science teachers to assign some physics experiments.
○ Join a science club or start one at your school.
○ Enter a project in a science fair. If your school does not sponsor science fairs, you may find fairs sponsored by your school district, your state, or a science society.
○ Talk to a physicist about his or her career. Ask your science teacher or counselor to help you set up an interview.

Physicists at Fermi National Accelerator Laboratory conduct an experiment. (Reidar Hahn, Fermi National Accelerator Laboratory)

FOR MORE INFO

For employment statistics and information on jobs and career planning, contact
American Institute of Physics
One Physics Ellipse
College Park, MD 20740-3843
Tel: 301-209-3100
E-mail: aipinfo@aip.org
http://www.aip.org

American Physical Society
One Physics Ellipse
College Park, MD 20740-3844
Tel: 301-209-3200
http://www.aps.org

Fermilab offers information on internships, employment opportunities, and an overview of its laboratory at its Web site.
Fermi National Accelerator Laboratory
Education Office
PO Box 500
Batavia, IL 60510-0500
Tel: 630-840-3092
http://www.fnal.gov

from less than $52,070 to $143,570 or more. Physicists employed by the federal government had mean earnings of $102,920 in 2006. The most highly paid physicists have doctoral degrees and many years of experience.

Outlook

Employment for physicists should grow more slowly than the average, according to the U.S. Department of Labor. Increases in government research, particularly in the Departments of Defense and Energy, and in private-sector research, will create more opportunities for physicists, but there will be stiff competition among Ph.D. holders for basic positions. The need to replace workers who retire will account for almost all new job openings.

Software Designers

What Software Designers Do

Software is the set of codes that tells a computer what to do. It comes in the form of the familiar packaged software that you find in a computer store. Software also comes in special forms designed for the specific needs of a particular business. *Software designers* create these software programs, also called applications. *Computer programmers* then create the software by writing the code that gives instructions to the computer.

Software designers must imagine every detail of what a software application will do, how it will do it, and how it will appear on the screen. An example is how a home accounting program is created. The software designer first decides what the program should be able to do, such as balance a checkbook, keep track of incoming and outgoing bills, and keep records of expenses. For each of these tasks, the software designer decides what menus and icons to use, and what each screen will look like. For example, the designer may want the part of the program with expense records to produce a pie chart that shows the percentage of each household expense in the overall household budget.

Some software companies build custom-designed software for the specific needs or problems of one business. Some

What Is Software?

The term *software* was coined to differentiate it from *hardware*, which is the physical parts of the computer system.

There are three types of software. *System software* controls a computer's internal functioning, usually through an operating system, and runs such extras as monitors, printers, and storage devices. *Application software* directs the computer to carry out commands given by the user. Application software includes word processing, spreadsheet, database management, inventory, and payroll programs. *Network software* coordinates communication between the computers that are linked in a network.

EXPLORING

○ Learn as much as you can about computers.

○ Keep up with new technology by reading computer magazines and by talking to other computer users.

○ Join computer clubs.

○ Surf the Internet for more information about this field.

○ Advanced students can put their design/programming knowledge to work by designing and programming their own applications, such as simple games and utility programs.

businesses are large enough that they employ software designers on staff who create software applications for their computer systems.

Education and Training

Computer, science, and math classes will prepare you for a career as a software designer. In high school, you should take as many of these courses as possible.

To be a software designer, you will need a bachelor's degree in computer science plus at least one year of experience with a programming language. You also need knowledge of the field for which you will be designing software. For example, someone with a bachelor's degree in computer science with a minor in business or accounting has an excellent chance for employment in creating business and accounting software.

Earnings

Median salaries for computer and information scientists (a job category that includes software designers) were $93,950 in 2006, according to the U.S. Department of Labor. Salaries ranged from less than $53,590 to $144,880 or more annually. At the managerial level, salaries are even higher and can reach $160,000 or more.

Outlook

Jobs in software design are expected to grow much faster than the average, according to the U.S. Department of Labor. Employment of computing professionals is expected to

Math Whizzes

○ Maria Gaetana Agnesi (1718–1799) was known for her discussion of the cubic curve and was called the Witch of Agnesi.

○ Archimedes (c. 287–212 B.C.) was a Greek mathematician and inventor. He was known for his work in mechanics and hydrostatics.

○ Euclid (c. 300 B.C.) was a Greek geometer whose main work, *Elements*, was a chief source of geometrical reasoning and methods until the 19th century.

○ Sophie Germain (1776–1831) was a French mathematician who contributed to the study of acoustics and elasticity and the theory of numbers.

○ Blaise Pascal (1623–1662) was a French scientist and philosopher. At 16 he wrote an original paper on conic sections. He also invented a mechanical calculator, the syringe, and the hydraulic press.

Source: *Funk & Wagnalls New Encyclopedia*

increase as technology advances. The expanding use of the Internet by businesses has caused a growing need for skilled professionals.

FOR MORE INFO

For information on career opportunities for women in computing, contact
Association for Women in Computing
41 Sutter Street, Suite 1006
San Francisco, CA 94104-4903
Tel: 415-905-4663
E-mail: info@awc-hq.org
http://www.awc-hq.org

For information on computer careers and student programs, contact
IEEE Computer Society

1730 Massachusetts Avenue NW
Washington, DC 20036-1992
Tel: 202-371-0101
http://www.computer.org

For industry information, contact
Software & Information Industry Association
1090 Vermont Avenue NW, Sixth Floor
Washington, DC 20005-4095
Tel: 202-289-7442
http://www.siia.net

Software Engineers

What Software Engineers Do

Businesses use computers to do complicated work for them. In many cases, their needs are so specialized that commercial software programs cannot perform the desired tasks. *Software engineers* change existing software or create new software to solve problems in many fields, including business, medicine, law, communications, aerospace, and science.

The projects software engineers work on are all different, but their methods for solving a problem are similar. First, engineers talk to clients to find out their needs and to define the problems they are having. Next, the engineers look at the software already used by the client to see whether it could be changed or if an entirely new system is needed. When they have all the facts, software engineers use scientific methods and mathematical models to figure out possible solutions to the problems. Then they choose the best solution and prepare a written proposal for managers and other engineers.

Once a proposal is accepted, software engineers and technicians check with hardware engineers to make sure computers are powerful enough to run the new programs. The software engineers then outline the program details. *Engineering technicians* write the initial version in computer languages.

Where Do They Work?

Most software engineers are employed by computer systems design and related services companies and by consulting firms. Software engineers also work in the following industries:

- software publishing
- medicine
- industry
- government/military
- communications
- aerospace
- science
- engineering firms

Throughout the programming process, engineers and technicians run diagnostic tests on the program to make sure it is working well at every stage. They also meet regularly with the client to make sure they are meeting their goals and to learn about any changes the client may want.

When a software project is complete, the engineer prepares a demonstration of it for the client. Software engineers might also install the program, train users, and make arrangements to help with any problems that arise in the future.

Education and Training

Take as many computer, math, and science courses as possible in high school. Classes that rely on schematic drawing and flowcharts are also very valuable. English and speech courses will help you improve your communication skills, which are very important for software engineers.

As more and more well-educated professionals have entered the industry, most employers now require a bachelor's degree.

EXPLORING

○ Learn as much as you can about computers, computer software, and computer hardware.
○ Read computer magazines and talk to other computer users.
○ Join computer clubs and surf the Internet for information about working in this field.
○ Try to spend a day with a working software engineer in order to experience the field firsthand. Your school guidance counselor or teacher can help you arrange such a visit.

Computer Trivia

○ The late John Tukey, professor of statistics at Princeton, coined the terms "software" and "bit."
○ The first hard drive available for the Apple had a capacity of 5 megabytes.
○ The average mouse pad is $8^{3}/_{4}$" by $7^{1}/_{2}$".

FOR MORE INFO

For information on internships, student membership, and the student magazine, Crossroads, *contact*
Association for Computing Machinery
2 Penn Plaza, Suite 701
New York, NY 10121-0701
Tel: 212-626-0500
http://www.acm.org

For information on career opportunities for women in computing, contact
Association for Women in Computing
41 Sutter Street, Suite 1006
San Francisco, CA 94104-4903
Tel: 415-905-4663
E-mail: info@awc-hq.org
http://www.awc-hq.org

For information on computer careers and student programs, contact
IEEE Computer Society
1730 Massachusetts Avenue NW
Washington, DC 20036-1992
Tel: 202-371-0101
http://www.computer.org

For industry information, contact
Software & Information Industry Association
1090 Vermont Avenue NW, Sixth Floor
Washington, DC 20005-4095
Tel: 202-289-7442
http://www.siia.net

A typical degree concentration for an applications software engineer is software engineering or computer science. Systems software engineers typically pursue a concentration in computer science or computer information systems.

Earnings

Software engineers with a bachelor's degree in computer engineering earned starting salaries of $52,464 in 2005, according to the National Association of Colleges and Employers. New computer engineers with a master's degree averaged $60,354. Salaries for software engineers ranged from less than $49,350 to more than $125,750 per year. Experienced software engineers can earn over $150,000 a year. Software engineers generally earn more in areas where there is a high concentration of computer companies, such as the Silicon Valley in northern California.

Outlook

Software engineering is one of the fastest-growing occupations in the United States. Computer companies, consulting firms, major corporations, insurance agencies, banks, and countless other industries hire software engineers.

Statisticians

What Statisticians Do

Statisticians use mathematics and statistical theory to collect and interpret information in a particular field. Most statisticians work in one of three kinds of jobs: They may teach and research at a university, they may work in a governmental agency (such as the U.S. Census Bureau), or they may work in a business or industry. Some statisticians work for public opinion research companies.

Statisticians usually specialize in one of two areas. *Mathematical statisticians* think of new statistical methods and theories and create new ways to use these theories. *Applied statisticians* apply existing formulas to new questions. They may try to predict population growth or future economic conditions.

In some cases, statisticians actually go out and gather the statistics they need. More often, people who are trained especially in fact-gathering techniques collect such facts, which statisticians then organize and analyze.

Education and Training

Statisticians must have strong mathematics and computer backgrounds. In high school, you will need to take college-preparatory classes in mathematics, statistics, and computer science.

A bachelor's degree is the minimum education you need to work as a statistician. For many positions, you will need a

Did You Know?

Currently, there are about 19,000 statisticians in the United States. About 20 percent work for the federal government. The others work in state and local governments, in industry (especially in scientific research and development services, the insurance industry, and pharmaceutical and medicine manufacturing), or as teachers and researchers at colleges and universities. Jobs for statisticians can be found throughout the country, but most of them are in larger cities.

EXPLORING

○ Read books and magazines about math and statistics.

○ Ask your math teachers to show you a statistics textbook. They might be able to give you some simple statistical problems related to grades, for example.

○ Ask your math teacher or guidance counselor to arrange a visit to a local insurance agency, the local office of the Internal Revenue Service, or a nearby college to talk to people who use statistical methods.

master's or doctoral degree. In college, many students choose a major in mathematics, or in the field they hope to work in, such as chemistry or sociology.

Earnings

The U.S. Department of Labor reports that the median annual salary for all statisticians was $65,720 in 2006. Salaries ranged from less than $37,010 to more than $108,630 annually. The National Association of Colleges and Employers reports that starting-salary offers for mathematics and statistics graduates averaged $43,448 a year in 2005. Statisticians employed by the federal government earned mean annual salaries of $85,460 in 2006.

Outlook

The number of jobs in this field is not expected to grow very much in the next decade. However, statisticians with advanced

What Does Florence Nightingale Have to Do with Statistics?

You probably know Florence Nightingale (1820–1910) as a famous nurse and pioneer in British health care reform. Did you know that she was also a statistician? When she was serving as a nurse during the Crimean War, she collected data using statistical techniques to find out how many British soldiers died because of unsanitary hospital conditions. She used this information to show why hospital conditions needed to be changed. By doing this, Florence Nightingale showed how statistics can be used to improve medical and surgical practices.

What Do Sports Statisticians Do?

Sports statisticians compute and record the statistics on a particular sports event. They use basic math and algebra and calculators and computers. Most high school, college, and professional sports teams have an official scorer/statistician who attends every home game and sits courtside, at what is called the scorer's table. The statistician is also called the *official scorer* because if anyone questions any item on the scoreboard, the statistician is the one who provides the answer.

Many statisticians still work by hand with a special notebook for recording the game statistics. As each play and call occurs in the game, the statistician writes down the play or call in a particular column or row of the stat book. Later, the statistician will add the total number of player errors, rebounds, assists, or goals. He or she can use these numbers to calculate such statistics as the average number of rebounds in a quarter or per game. Usually, the statistician keeps the stats by individual for both the home team and the visiting team. At the end of the game, the statistician can then provide both coaches and teams with specific information on their play during the game.

degrees or specialized training in computer science, engineering, or finance should have good opportunities. Many of the current openings are in scientific and medical research.

FOR MORE INFO

For career information, contact
American Statistical Association
732 North Washington Street
Alexandria, VA 22314-1943
Tel: 888-231-3473
E-mail: asainfo@amstat.org
http://www.amstat.org

Society for Industrial and Applied Mathematics
3600 Market Street, 6th Floor
Philadelphia, PA 19104-2688
Tel: 215-382-9800
http://www.siam.org

Surveyors

What Surveyors Do

Surveyors use a variety of mechanical and electronic tools to measure exact distances and locate positions on the Earth's surface. These geographic measurements are used in many ways. They determine property boundaries and provide information for mapmaking and construction and engineering projects. Wherever you may need to find exact locations and measure points, surveyors can make an accurate and detailed survey of the area.

Some surveyors work on proposed construction projects such as highways, airstrips, housing developments, and bridges to provide the necessary measurements before the engineers and construction crews begin work. Some help mapmakers chart unexplored areas. Others survey land claims, bodies of water, and underground mines. Some clear the right-of-way for water pipes, drainage ditches, or telecommunications lines. Some surveyors measure areas of land, sea, or space that are so large that their measurements must take into account the curvature of the Earth. Some use special photographic equipment installed in airplanes or ground stations to chart areas that are hard to reach in person.

Whatever their area of specialization, surveyors work 40-hour weeks except when overtime is necessary to meet a project deadline. The peak work period is during the summer months when weather conditions are most favorable. However, it is not uncommon for the

A surveyor uses a transit to help complete a survey for a new highway. (C.W. McKeen, The Image Works)

surveyor to be exposed to demanding weather conditions such as extreme heat or cold, rain, snow, or high winds.

Education and Training

It is important to concentrate on math classes to prepare for a surveying career. In high school, you should take courses in algebra, geometry, physics, and mechanical drawing. After high school, you will have to complete a four-year college program in surveying or engineering. Civil engineering, with a surveying emphasis, is a common major. To advance in some of the more technical specialties, you may have to pursue study beyond a bachelor's degree.

Earnings

In 2006, surveyors earned a median annual salary of $48,290, according to

EXPLORING

○ While in high school, begin to familiarize yourself with terms, projects, and tools used in this profession by reading books and magazines on the topic. One magazine you can read online is *Professional Surveyor Magazine* at http://www.profsurv.com.

○ Learn all you can about these subjects: information technology, mathematics, computers, computer graphics, satellite technology, working outdoors, the environment, science, and travel.

○ Ask your teacher or counselor to help you arrange an interview with a professional surveyor.

To Be a Successful Surveyor, You Should . . .

○ have the ability to visualize and understand objects in two and three dimensions (spatial relationships)

○ have the ability to discriminate between and compare shapes, sizes, lines, shadings, and other forms (form perception)

○ be able to work with a variety of mechanical and electronic measuring devices

○ be a good leader (since you will direct and supervise members of a surveying team)

○ enjoy working outdoors in all kinds of weather

What Do Surveying and Mapping Technicians Do?

Surveying and mapping technicians help civil engineers, mapmakers, and professional surveyors determine, describe, and record geographic areas and features. Surveying and mapping technicians set up, adjust, and take readings from delicate surveying instruments. Some technicians adjust and operate instruments called theodolites, which measure vertical and horizontal angles of land or buildings. Some technicians use equipment that electronically measures distances, or they may have to rely on measuring tape and chains. As readings are taken, the technicians must keep careful notes so that the surveying reports will be accurate. They often enter the information from readings into computers.

Technicians may also do highway, pipeline, railway, or powerline surveying. Technicians who work for hydrographic surveying firms make surveys of bodies of water. These surveys help engineers to plan breakwaters, dams, locks, piers, and bridges.

Mining companies also hire surveying and mapping technicians. These technicians use instruments that set the boundaries of mining claims and also show features of the Earth that indicate the presence of valuable natural resources.

Topographical surveys show such features as mountains, lakes, forests, farms, and other landmarks. Technicians who do topographical surveying often take aerial and land photographs with special cameras that photograph large areas of land.

Education and Training: Surveying and mapping technicians must take a two-year program in surveying and mapping at a junior college or technical school. Surveying firms often provide additional on-the-job training.

Earnings: The average yearly salary for full-time technicians is about $32,000 a year. Some earn more than $53,000 a year.

Outlook: Job opportunities for surveying and mapping technicians should be good through the next decade.

the U.S. Department of Labor. Salaries ranged from less than $26,690 to $79,910 or more a year. In general, the federal government paid the highest mean wages to its surveyors, $72,180 a year in 2006.

Outlook

The employment outlook for surveyors is expected to be fairly good in the near future. The widespread use of technology, such as the Global Positioning System and Geographic Information Systems, will provide jobs to surveyors with strong technical and computer skills. Growth in urban and suburban areas (with the need for new streets, homes, shopping centers, schools, and gas and water lines); state and federal highway improvement programs; and local urban redevelopment programs also will provide employment opportunities.

FOR MORE INFO

For information on surveying careers, contact
American Congress on Surveying and Mapping
6 Montgomery Village Avenue, Suite 403
Gaithersburg, MD 20879-3557
Tel: 240-632-9716
E-mail: info@acsm.net
http://www.acsm.net

For information on awards and recommended books to read, contact the following organizations or check out their Web sites
American Association for Geodetic Surveying
6 Montgomery Village Avenue, Suite 403
Gaithersburg, MD 20879-3557
Tel: 240-632-9716
http://www.aagsmo.org

National Society of Professional Surveyors
6 Montgomery Village Avenue, Suite 403
Gaithersburg, MD 20879-3557
Tel: 240-632-9716
http://www.nspsmo.org

For information on photogrammetry and careers in the field, contact
American Society for Photogrammetry and Remote Sensing
5410 Grosvenor Lane, Suite 210
Bethesda, MD 20814-2160
Tel: 301-493-0290
E-mail: asprs@asprs.org
http://www.asprs.org

Glossary

accredited approved as meeting established standards for providing good training and education; this approval is usually given by an independent organization of professionals

apprentice a person who is learning a trade by working under the supervision of a skilled worker; apprentices often receive classroom instruction in addition to their supervised practical experience

associate's degree an academic rank or title granted by a community or junior college or similar institution to graduates of a two-year program of education beyond high school

bachelor's degree an academic rank or title given to a person who has completed a four-year program of study at a college or university; also called an undergraduate degree or baccalaureate

career an occupation for which a worker receives training and has an opportunity for advancement

certified approved as meeting established requirements for skill, knowledge, and experience in a particular field; people are certified by the organization of professionals in their field

college a higher education institution that is above the high school level

community college a public or private two-year college attended by students who do not usually live at the college; graduates of a community college receive an associate's degree and may transfer to a four-year college or university to complete a bachelor's degree

diploma a certificate or document given by a school to show that a person has completed a course of study or has graduated from the school

distance education a type of educational program that allows students to take classes and complete their education by mail or the Internet

doctorate the highest academic rank or title granted by a graduate school to a person who has completed a program after having received a master's degree

fringe benefit a payment or benefit to an employee in addition to regular wages or salary; examples of fringe benefits include a pension, a paid vacation, and health or life insurance

graduate school a school that people may attend after they have received their bachelor's degree; people who complete an educational program at a graduate school earn a master's degree or a doctorate

intern an advanced student (usually one with at least some college training) in a professional field who is employed in a job that is intended to provide supervised practical experience for the student

internship 1. the position or job of an intern. 2. the period of time when a person is an intern

junior college a two-year college that offers courses like those in the first half of a four-year college program; graduates of a junior college usually receive an associate's degree and may transfer to a four-year college or university to complete a bachelor's degree

liberal arts the subjects covered by college courses that develop broad general knowledge rather than specific occupational skills; the liberal arts are often considered to include philosophy, literature and the arts, history, language, and some courses in the social sciences and natural sciences

licensed having formal permission from the proper authority to carry out an activity that would be illegal without that permission; for example, a person must be licensed to practice medicine or drive a car

major (in college) the academic field in which a student specializes and receives a degree

master's degree an academic rank or title granted by a graduate school to a person who has completed a program after having received a bachelor's degree

pension an amount of money paid regularly by an employer to a former employee after he or she retires from working

scholarship a gift of money to a student to help the student pay for further education

social studies courses of study (such as civics, geography, and history) that deal with how human societies work

starting salary annual pay for a newly hired employee; the starting salary is usually a smaller amount than is paid to a more experienced worker

technical college a private or public college offering two- or four-year programs in technical subjects; technical colleges offer courses in both general and technical subjects and award associate's degrees and bachelor's degrees

technician a worker with specialized practical training in a mechanical or scientific subject who works under the supervision of scientists, engineers, or other professionals; technicians typically receive two years of college-level education after high school

technologist a worker in a mechanical or scientific field with more training than a technician; technologists typically must have between two and four years of college-level education after high school

undergraduate a student at a college or university who has not yet received a degree

undergraduate degree See **bachelor's degree**

union an organization whose members are workers in a particular industry or company; the union works to gain better wages, benefits, and working conditions for its members; also called a labor union or trade union

vocational school a public or private school that offers training in one or more skills or trades

wage money that is paid in return for work done, especially money paid on the basis of the number of hours or days worked

Index of Job Titles

Browse and Learn More

Books

Burnett, Rebecca. *Careers for Number Crunchers & Other Quantitative Types.* 2d ed. New York: McGraw-Hill, 2002.

Clemens, Meg, Sean Glenn, Glenn Clemens, and Sean Clemens. *The Everything Kids' Math Puzzles Book: Brain Teasers, Games, and Activities for Hours of Fun.* Cincinnati, Ohio: Adams Media Corporation, 2003

Eberts, Marjorie, and Margaret Gisler. *Careers for Computer Buffs & Other Technological Types.* 3d ed. New York: McGraw-Hill, 2006.

Enzensberger, Hans Magnus, Rotraut Susanne Berner, and Michael Henry Heim. *The Number Devil: A Mathematical Adventure.* New York: Owl Books, 2000.

Fitzgerald, Theresa R. *Math Dictionary for Kids: The Essential Guide to Math Terms, Strategies, and Tables.* Waco, Tex.: Prufrock Press, 2005.

Gralla, Preston. *How the Internet Works.* 8th ed. Indianapolis, Ind.: Que Publishing, 2006.

Kraynak, Joe. *The Complete Idiot's Guide to Computer Basics.* 4th ed. New York: Alpha, 2007.

Lambert, Stephen, and Ruth DeCotis. *Great Jobs for Math Majors.* 2d ed. New York: McGraw-Hill, 2005.

Long, Lynette. *Math Smarts: Tips, Tricks, and Secrets for Making Math More Fun!* Middleton, Wisc.: American Girl, 2004.

Peterson's Summer Opportunities for Kids & Teenagers 2007. 24th ed. Lawrenceville, N.J.: Peterson's, 2006.

Salvadori, Mario. *The Art of Construction: Projects and Principles for Beginning Engineers and Architects.* 3d ed. Chicago: Chicago Review Press, 2000.

Sterrett, Andrew (ed.). *101 Careers in Mathematics*. 2nd ed. Washington, D.C.: Mathematical Association of America, 2003.

VanCleave, Janice. *Janice VanCleave's Engineering for Every Kid: Easy Activities That Make Learning Science Fun*. San Francisco: Jossey-Bass, 2007.

Vorderman, Carol. *How Math Works*. New York: Readers Digest, 1999.

Woods, Michael, and Mary B. Woods. *Ancient Machines: From Wedges to Waterwheels*. Minneapolis: Runestone Press, 1999.

Web Sites

A+ Math
http://www.aplusmath.com

AAA Math
http://www.aaamath.com

American Library Association: Great Web Sites for Kids
http://www.ala.org/greatsites

Brain Teasers
http://www.eduplace.com/math/brain

Computer History Museum
http://www.computerhistory.org

Coolmath.com
http://coolmath.com

Engineer Girl!
http://www.engineergirl.org

Fermilab: Education
http://www.fnal.gov/pub/education/k-12_programs.html

Indexes of Biographies
http://www-groups.dcs.st-and.ac.uk/~history/BiogIndex.html

Intro to Astronomy
http://www.astronomy.com/asy/default.aspx?c=ps&id=6

Invention Dimension
http://web.mit.edu/invent/invent-main.html

Investing for Kids
http://library.thinkquest.org/3096

Kids & Money
http://www.ext.nodak.edu/extnews/pipeline/d-parent.htm

Kids' Money Store
http://www.kidsmoneystore.com/

Math Cats
http://www.mathcats.com

Math Playground
http://www.MathPlayground.com

A Maths Dictionary for Kids
http://www.amathsdictionaryforkids.com

Measurements Converter
http://www.convert-me.com/en

Measuring the World Around Us: A High-Tech Career in Professional Surveying
http://www.acsm.net/surveyingcareer.html

National Aeronautics and Space Administration Kids' Club
http://www.nasa.gov/audience/forkids/home

National Inventors Hall of Fame
http://www.invent.org/hall_of_fame/1_0_0_hall_of_fame.asp

Optics For Teens: Get Bright
http://www.opticsforteens.org

PhysicsCentral
http://www.physicscentral.com

PhysicsQuest
http://www.physicscentral.com/physicsquest

Scientists in Action!
http://mac.usgs.gov/isb/pubs/booklets/scientists/index.html

Society of Exploration Geophysicists Student Connections
http://students.seg.org/kids

The Tech Museum of Innovation
http://www.thetech.org

U.S. Department of Energy: For Students and Kids
http://www.energy.gov/forstudentsandkids.htm

U.S. Mint H.I.P. Pocket Change
http://www.usmint.gov/kids

YoungInvestor.com
http://www.younginvestor.com